HENRY KISSINGER

By the same author

Journal d'un jeune diplomate dans l'Amérique de Trump
(Éditions Gallimard, 2018)
[Diary of a Young Diplomat in Trump's America]

Georges Pompidou, l'Intemporel (Éditions Gallimard, 2025)
[Georges Pompidou: A Timeless Figure]

As contributor

Grands Diplomates: Les maîtres des relations internationales de Mazarin à nos jours – edited by Hubert Védrine
(Éditions Perrin, 2024)
[Great Diplomats: The Masters of International Relations, From Mazarin Up Until Today]

HENRY KISSINGER

An Intimate Portrait of
the Master of Realpolitik

JÉRÉMIE GALLON

Translated By Roland Glasser

Profile Books

First published in Great Britain in 2025 by
Profile Books Ltd
29 Cloth Fair
London
EC1A 7JQ

www.profilebooks.com

Copyright © Jérémie Gallon, 2025
English language translation copyright © Roland Glasser, 2025

1 3 5 7 9 10 8 6 4 2

Typeset in Berling Nova Text by MacGuru Ltd
Printed and bound in Great Britain by
CPI Group (UK) Ltd, Croydon CR0 4YY

The moral right of the author has been asserted.

All rights reserved. Without limiting the rights under copyright reserved above, no part of this publication may be reproduced, stored or introduced into a retrieval system, or transmitted, in any form or by any means (electronic, mechanical, photocopying, recording or otherwise), without the prior written permission of both the copyright owner and the publisher of this book.

A CIP catalogue record for this book is available from the British Library.

We make every effort to make sure our products are safe for the purpose for which they are intended. For more information check our website or contact Authorised Rep Compliance Ltd., Ground Floor, 71 Lower Baggot Street, Dublin, D02 P593, Ireland, www.arccompliance.com

ISBN 978 1 80522 460 0

For my father

Contents

Foreword ix

De Gaulle 1
Football 11
Glamour 19
Harvard 29
Helsinki 39
Humour 47
Indefensible? 53
Jewishness 67
Lee Kuan Yew 75
Mentor 83
Metternich 89
Nixon 95
Paula 107
Realpolitik 111
Refugee 121
Rockefeller 127
Sadat 133
Teacher 145
Zhou Enlai 151
Conclusion 159
Epilogue 165

Chronology 177
Selective bibliography 183
Acknowledgements 185
Notes 186
Index 203

Foreword

It was one of those winter days where Paris sat bathed in sunlight beneath a sky of cloudless blue, the air cold and crisp. I was sitting in a cosy living room overlooking the Théâtre de l'Odéon. Suddenly the friend I was with asked me: 'Why are you so interested in Kissinger, Jérémie? It's something I've wondered for a while now.'

It was a legitimate question. Over the previous year, he, like all my friends and family – not to mention my students – had counted the cost of the passion that gripped me at every discussion of the career and life of Henry Kissinger. Each time we met, I bombarded him with unsolicited anecdotes regarding the former US secretary of state. But as I opened my mouth to explain precisely why, for the past few months, I had been spending every spare moment reading and writing about Kissinger, I didn't know where to begin.

As a teenager, I was already intrigued by the man whom some people had no hesitation in mentioning in the same breath as those great diplomats, Talleyrand and Metternich. I knew next to nothing of his life, yet I had the faint intuition that Henry Kissinger was one of those rare contemporary figures to have 'written' history with a capital H. Above all, he embodied a word – 'diplomacy' – that fired my imagination. Indeed, his book *Diplomacy* had pride of place in my bedroom.

Leaving aside the intellectual and political legacy of this statesman, there was something fascinating about the man himself. Henry Kissinger was one of those exceptional humans capable of turning their life into a novel. A novel in which a man's faults, fragilities, failures and triumphs appear endlessly entwined with History itself.

There is something extraordinary about the life journey of this little Jewish boy from Germany who was born just outside Nuremberg, grew up in the very heart of Nazism and went on to become the greatest diplomat the United States has ever known.

Fate may have placed this child in the lion's den, but he would become the man who toppled regimes, forged alliances that would alter the global balance of powers and lastingly reshaped the geopolitical chessboard of the twentieth century.

Thirteen members of his family were murdered in the death camps. He returned to the land of his birth wearing an American army uniform to fight Hitler's regime and denazify the country he'd had to flee in fear.

He first set foot in New York as a penniless fifteen-year-old refugee in late summer 1938. Thirty-five years later, he would take the oath of office as secretary of state in the gilded halls of the White House.

Recipient of the Nobel Peace Prize and the admiration of an entire nation, he would spend his entire life plagued by a deep sense of insecurity, which would often take him to the verge of paranoia.

Henry Kissinger's life also says much about a country, the United States of America, where I studied and then lived. A country that I loved more and more as I explored it, and which remains very dear to me – despite the division, the fear and the fury that gnaw away at it.

The United States became the leading twentieth-century superpower because it was a place where a young German Jewish refugee could, through his work ethic and his character, attain one of the highest offices. If you're seeking the roots of American power, look no further than this country's

Foreword

extraordinary capability to nourish itself with the greatest talents in the world, while also enabling those individuals to express their full potential. In fact, it is striking that three of the greatest American diplomats of the second half of the twentieth century – Madeleine Albright, Zbigniew Brzeziński and Henry Kissinger – were immigrants. This exceptional trio, who helped shape American power and were tireless defenders of the nation's interests, were all born in the heart of Europe.

For a long time, America had the self-confidence to give immigrants from across the world their chance, enabling the country to become an empire that dominated the world politically, economically, technologically and culturally. But having withdrawn into itself these past few years, having given in to the fear of the other and forgotten what made it great, American power now faces a grim future. The day when it will no longer be possible for a young Henry Kissinger – whether from Guatemala, Syria or Eritrea – to become a future secretary of state is the day that the United States will have fallen into an inexorable decline.

But the primary reason for my fascination with the life of Henry Kissinger is that it carries so many lessons for Europe, the continent where I'm from and the cradle of a political project that I consider to be both the most precious and the most fragile.

The most important teaching of Kissinger's life is that when Europe yields to the sort of vehement nationalism and hatred – chief of which is antisemitism – that still plague it today, it deprives itself of some of its most talented children, denying them the opportunity to accomplish their innate potential and therefore condemning them to exile. There is something tragic in the fact that it was not in the service of Europe that Henry Kissinger deployed his vast talents, despite being born in the heart of the continent.

Kissinger's life is also a ceaseless reminder that if Europe wishes to avoid disappearing into the dustbin of history, then it must finally equip itself with a diplomacy worthy of the name. This means that at a time when the European Union is gripped between the national egotisms of its member states and third powers that no longer hide their desire to weaken or even kill it, the need for a European *Realpolitik* has never been more pressing. 'A country that demands moral perfection in its foreign policy', wrote Kissinger, 'will achieve neither perfection nor security.'[1] If we continue to restrict ourselves to a simulacrum of foreign policy – one that all too often is muddled with an idealism that is nothing but the mask of our own cowardice – then we will condemn ourselves to collapse.

Where are the Richelieus, Bismarcks, Metternichs and Kissingers of today who could mould Europe into a twenty-first-century power? The European Union is fortunate to have a European diplomatic service. It now needs to be empowered with the people and the strategic vision to enable Europe finally to be an actor in the evolution of the world and no longer merely a spectator.

This may seem an inaccessible dream to many. But as the student Kissinger wrote so superbly about Metternich: 'For men become myths, not by what they know, nor even by what they achieve, but by the tasks they set for themselves.'[2] The time is therefore nigh for Europeans to dream great things for Europe once more.

Still, despite the many reasons that led me, a young and passionate European, to interest myself in Henry Kissinger, I do not ignore the mistakes, the personal faults or the grey areas that marked his life.

I do not ignore that Kissinger oversaw a bombing campaign of Cambodia and Laos, which caused the death of hundreds of thousands of civilians, and during which more bombs were dropped by American planes than by the Allies during the whole of the Second World War. I do not ignore the constant support that the Nixon administration afforded to Pakistan

Foreword

– accused by many of having perpetrated a massacre in Bangladesh in 1971.[3] I do not ignore the American backing provided to General Pinochet during both the military coup that brought him to power in Chile in 1973 and the repression that followed. And nor do I ignore the approval given by the Ford administration to the brutal invasion of East Timor by Indonesia in 1975. These are indelible stains on the legacy of Henry Kissinger.

But whatever the moral judgement that each of us is free to make about the man, I remain convinced that Kissinger's life, his relationship to history, his vision of foreign policy and his writings have left a trace that will linger long after his death. And in that trace, we Europeans may find many of the answers to some of the major challenges facing us.

Given the plethora of books that have been written about Henry Kissinger, this one has no ambition to be a new biography. I am neither a historian nor an academic; I do not claim to give an exhaustive account of Kissinger's contradictions, his exceptional intelligence, and the twists and turns of his career. In the following pages I seek only to sketch the intellectual portrait of a man who left a deep mark on me. A man who – despite the many shades of grey that colour his life – I am convinced may be a huge source of inspiration for all those wishing to build the European diplomacy of tomorrow.

De Gaulle

Henry Kissinger harboured big ambitions when he arrived in Paris on 28 February 1969. He had just taken up his post as national security advisor and hoped that Nixon's three-day trip to the French capital would mark the start of a new relationship between the two countries. After a decade of strained relations, with Charles de Gaulle taking a defiant stance vis-à-vis the United States, Kissinger felt that the time had come to mend fences with this key, yet difficult, ally.

It would be an understatement to say that the 1960s were a time of recurring tensions between Paris and Washington. First, John F. Kennedy saw de Gaulle shoot down his grand plan for a transatlantic partnership between the United States of America and the 'United States of Europe'.[1] Then France refused to sign the Partial Test Ban Treaty of 1963. And no one in Washington forgot that it was the Gaullists who, in an improbable alliance with the Communists, torpedoed the dream of a European army in 1954. Following the failure of the European Defence Community, Charles de Gaulle then opposed a project (which had the support of the White House) to create a Multilateral Force comprising a naval nuclear deterrent crewed by personnel from multiple NATO members.

It is striking that the United States at the time unreservedly supported the project to build a European army. Washington saw this initiative as complementary to, rather than competing with, NATO. Even more importantly, the American leadership viewed a European army as being a prerequisite to the rebirth of European power, itself a precondition to the strengthening of the transatlantic relationship.[2]

Henry Kissinger

When he came to power in 1963, Lyndon B. Johnson also reproached de Gaulle for failing to continue the legacy of the founding fathers of European integration. He detected in the new Franco-German relationship a cloaked strategy to isolate the United Kingdom. Indeed, the French leader's veto in January 1963 of Britain's request to join the European Economic Community was very poorly received in Washington. De Gaulle was perceived as an obstacle both to European integration and to the strengthening of the transatlantic relationship – two ambitions that American leaders viewed as intrinsically linked.

In this context, the decisions taken by Paris in 1966 to withdraw from both the gold-dollar standard and NATO's integrated command structure were no surprise to Lyndon B. Johnson. But they fuelled his exasperation with the French president, an exasperation that reached its peak when Charles de Gaulle firmly condemned the American intervention in Vietnam in his famous speech in Phnom Penh in September 1966. The fact that he predicted a very heavy defeat for the Americans was less than appreciated in the corridors of the White House.

Amid the chorus of disapproval voiced at Charles de Gaulle in the United States, there was one exception: Henry Kissinger. In an article for *Harper's* published in March 1965, entitled 'The illusionist: why we misread de Gaulle', he tried to explain what guided the French president's foreign policy.[3] According to Kissinger, it was a mistake to see any kind of anti-Americanism in de Gaulle's declarations and positions.

For Kissinger, it was clear that de Gaulle considered the United States to be France's indispensable ally. During periods of extreme tension with Moscow – be it when an American spy plane was shot down over Russia in May 1960, the construction of the Berlin Wall in August 1961 or the Cuban Missile Crisis in summer 1962 – the French president supported the United States without an ounce of hesitation. Kissinger also pointed out that there were many subjects, notably those related to the Cold War and the stance to be taken vis-à-vis Soviet power, where there were no major strategic divergences between France and the United States.

But de Gaulle was an ally who could not accept his country and Europe becoming an American protectorate. The French president had assigned himself the role, according to Kissinger, of 'teach[ing] his people and perhaps his Continent attitudes of independence and self-reliance'.[4] A transatlantic relationship or a supranational body that would constrain Europe and France too rigidly was not compatible with the feeling of grandeur that he wished to impart to the French people. It was therefore to reinspire his country and give his fellow citizens 'a specifically French sense of purpose'[5] that de Gaulle pursued the vision of an independent foreign policy.

Kissinger had already set out a similar analysis in an article headlined 'Strains on the Alliance', published in *Foreign Affairs* in January 1963. 'We have treated what is essentially a political and psychological problem as if it were primarily technical,' he wrote, before going on to say: 'We have shown little understanding for the concerns of some of our European allies that their survival should depend entirely on decisions made 3,000 miles away.'[6]

For the man who was still a Harvard professor, the major error committed by the Kennedy and Johnson administrations was having judged de Gaulle's policies without seeking to understand the historical context of his actions and the psychology of the French nation. In particular, he reminds the reader that although the United States and France shared the status of victor in 1945, this masked two quite different realities on either side of the Atlantic.

For America, the end of the Second World War marked the high point of its political, economic and military power. Conversely, despite de Gaulle having succeeded in hauling his country far enough to earn a place at the victors' table, France was not invited to either Yalta or Potsdam. Consumed by the question of decline, the French knew deep down that they were part of a Europe that was no longer the global centre of gravity. Kissinger understood that this was one of the reasons why France clung so fiercely to the remnants of a colonial empire, the last symbol of a bygone and much-missed power. In this context, the Americans were making a mistake by reacting so vehemently to Gaullist initiatives. They must realise that de Gaulle, like his people, could not be content with a bipolar world in which Europe would no longer be a main player in the march of history. This meant allowing France 'to regain – wherever possible – the right of independent decision'.[7]

However, it was not only the work undertaken by Kissinger to understand the motivations of Gaullist foreign policy that made a Franco-American rapprochement in 1969 possible. This development also grew out of the close personal relations forged between Nixon and de Gaulle over several years.

The two leaders met for the first time in April 1960, when Nixon was Eisenhower's vice president. Then, during the American's own spell in the wilderness, the French president received Nixon on two occasions, in 1963 and 1967.

The two men admired each other and shared common views on many subjects. A little over a year before Nixon's election to the White House, de Gaulle painted a flattering portrait of him to the US Military Attaché in Paris, Vernon Walters, confidently predicting that Nixon would become president one day, but noting that 'Mr Nixon, like me, will have been an exile in his own country.'[8] On 28 February 1969, at a dinner at the Elysée Palace in honour of the US president, de Gaulle again expressed his friendly feelings towards his American counterpart, insisting on the strength of the Franco-American relationship. To those who would accuse him of anti-Americanism, de Gaulle declared that although the United States and France are 'two countries naturally different in their situation, size and interests', they are 'drawn together by a two-centuries-old friendship, as well as by the profound community of a certain human ideal whose flame has often spread more light and warmth in both our countries than anywhere else on our earth'.[9] In response, Nixon paid de Gaulle fulsome homage, calling the French president 'a leader who has become a giant among men because he had courage, because he had vision, and because he had the wisdom that the world now seeks to solve its difficult problems'.[10]

But beyond the declarations and symbolic gestures, the French and American leaders would use this visit, which took place from 28 February to 2 March 1969, to attempt to make joint progress on several major areas. There were three in particular where Kissinger felt that, rather than being an obstacle, Charles de Gaulle could help resolve a number of challenges faced by the United States. These three areas were none other than the three pillars of American foreign policy that Kissinger wished to implement.

To understand these three pillars, we should remember that Kissinger had long studied Bismarck (initially as a student and later as a professor). Notably, he drew the conclusion that the genius of the Iron Chancellor lay in his ability to foster a system of alliances with powers whom his peers considered incompatible with each other. It was by simultaneously concluding an alliance with the Austro-Hungarian Empire and a secret Reinsurance Treaty with Tsarist Russia that Bismarck was able to extricate Prussia from its isolation.

Similarly, Kissinger thought that it would be possible for the United States to pursue three parallel foreign policy axes that hitherto appeared contradictory. He wanted to strengthen the transatlantic relationship, pursue a policy of Détente with the USSR and bring about a rapprochement with the China of Mao Zedong. His analysis of Gaullist foreign policy had convinced him that the French president could be a precious ally for all three.

For Kissinger, the strengthening of the transatlantic relationship should not be based on a deeper European integration. Breaking with the prevailing vision of the Kennedy and Johnson administrations, he thought that nation states would remain the key players in any European project and that Washington should therefore deepen relations with them. It would be through a policy of bilateral rapprochement, notably with France, that a strengthening of the transatlantic relationship would be possible. Kissinger's European vision, shared by Nixon, was music to de Gaulle's ears.

As regards the policy of Détente, Kissinger judged, correctly, that France would not be opposed to this in principle. He understood that de Gaulle, like most European leaders, wished only to avoid a rapprochement between Washington and Moscow becoming synonymous with a consolidation of blocs and a carving-up of the world to Europe's detriment. For Kissinger, the policy of Détente as he imagined it would, in fact, dovetail extremely well with the policy towards Russia and the Eastern Bloc pursued by the French president, who wished to establish a closer dialogue with the Kremlin.

Finally, Kissinger knew that he could count on the backing of Charles de Gaulle in a rapprochement with Beijing. The French president had long felt that the West should reach out to China in order to understand it better and to place it back on its spot on the geopolitical chessboard. The recognition of the People's Republic of China by France in January 1964 was studiously analysed by Kissinger and Nixon. Nixon recounted in his *Memoirs* how de Gaulle had told him: 'I do not feel that we should leave them [China] isolated in their rage. The West should try to get to know China, to have contacts, and to penetrate it. (...) It would be better for you to recognize China before you are obliged to do so by the growth of China.'[11]

During their ten hours of private meetings, Nixon and de Gaulle discussed these three areas at length. But another, unexpected subject also reared its head.

The first day of their visit, Kissinger hung back. He still lacked both the reputation and the aura that would soon come his way. But de Gaulle approached him. 'Why don't you get out of Vietnam?' the French president asked brusquely. Kissinger was momentarily speechless. Then he stammered: 'Because a sudden withdrawal might give us a credibility problem.' 'Where?' asked de Gaulle imperiously. 'In the Middle East,' replied Kissinger timidly, struggling to regain his habitual self-assurance. 'How very odd,' said de Gaulle with a sceptical tone. 'It is precisely in the Middle East that I thought your enemies had the credibility problem.' Then the French leader turned on his heel and began talking to another member of the delegation, the exchange with Kissinger over as fast as it had begun.[12]

The two men understood that the United States should extricate itself from the quagmire of Vietnam. But they disagreed on how to do so. De Gaulle felt that every day the American troops spent in Vietnam further weakened the world's leading superpower. It was not just a question of the thousands of young American lives being lost. The United States was also losing its greatest strength: its moral authority. A month later, at Eisenhower's funeral, de Gaulle and Nixon discussed the matter further. 'De Gaulle again urged that I take steps to put an end to the Vietnam War as quickly as possible,' Nixon later confided.[13]

Kissinger, however, felt that a sudden withdrawal on the part of the United States would send a negative signal to the rest of the world. Washington would lose the respect of all those who counted on the United States to stem the expansion of communism. He believed that American troops should respect a 'decent interval' of two or three years before withdrawing. Future events would prove that the American leaders would have been wise to follow the advice of their French ally.

Despite this disagreement, Nixon's trip to Paris, which ended on 2 March 1969, sealed the tightening of relations between France and the United States. It kicked off a three-year period during which Washington and Paris would coordinate much more closely. Nevertheless, it would soon be without Charles de Gaulle. On 28 April 1969, barely two months after his American counterpart's visit, the French president resigned. The special relationship between Nixon and de Gaulle would forever remain 'an unfinished symphony', to quote the historian Maurice Ferro.[14]

Although Kissinger spent very little time with de Gaulle while in office, the man who Nixon dubbed 'the giant' left a deep impression on him. In his account of his years at the White House, Kissinger sketches a laudatory portrait of the French president in just a few lines: 'He had performed the dramatic feats required by the crises that had brought him to power. He had consolidated new political institutions. He had achieved the decolonization of French Africa while maintaining French self-confidence at home and its prestige in the former colonies. Barely overcoming incipient civil war, he had restored French pride by giving it a central role in the policies of Europe and the Western Alliance. One of the principal purposes of his challenge to the United States was to inspire French self-assurance.'[15]

The rest of Kissinger's analysis is as interesting for what it conveys of his own vision of power as it is for his thoughts on the French leader. 'But the student upheavals of 1968 had shaken de Gaulle. And the challenges facing him thereafter were not of a magnitude he considered relevant to his vision of himself. To ensure a growing economy, to arbitrate contending claims on limited resources, to organize and manage a bureaucratic state – these were tasks for what he half-contemptuously called "quartermasters", not for heroic figures.'[16]

For Kissinger, de Gaulle was one of those very rare figures who leave their mark on history. But was he the man to submerge himself in the challenges inherent in the day-to-day stewarding of a country, the inner turmoil of political life, and the manoeuvrers of parties? No, the man who had saved France's honour was above all that. In this context: 'The referenda of April 17

[1969] provided the occasion for a dramatic departure instead of the slow erosion of authority that he so feared.'[17]

With this last sentence, Kissinger underlined the stark contrast between de Gaulle and the vast majority of our current leaders – those who, lacking the legitimacy that history had conferred upon de Gaulle, still try, each day, and with much political manoeuvring, to postpone the moment when they will have to leave office. Truly great men, in Kissinger's view, do not cling to power. For power is merely the means to enable the great man to change the course of history. Power without authority is worthless. And when authority starts to slip away, a sense of responsibility ought therefore to oblige a leader to step down.

At a conference held at Columbia University in April 1990 to commemorate the centenary of de Gaulle's birth, Kissinger described him as the 'true great man'. After talking at length about the man who 'had restored to France a certain vision of its identity and its prestige', Kissinger confessed: 'I have a great nostalgia for an American version of de Gaulle.'[18]

But Kissinger rued the fact that among Europe's leaders, too, there were no worthy heirs to the man whose moral and intellectual worth and 'strength of personality' he so admired. During an interview with *Der Spiegel* on 10 October 2005, Kissinger was asked which historical figure – Churchill or Bismarck – had left the deepest impression on him. Kissinger gave an answer that said it all: 'I have a lot of respect for Charles de Gaulle as well.' Then, doubling down on his appraisal of the former French president, he went on: 'In the period after the Second World War, there were still leaders in Europe who represented weak countries, but possessed a sense of global foreign policy.'[19]

For Kissinger, Charles de Gaulle would forever embody the 'man of character', an archetype defined by the French leader himself in *Le fil de l'épée* – a treatise on military leadership, written while he was still a young officer: 'Assured in his

Henry Kissinger

judgements and aware of his strength, he makes no concession to the desire to please. (...) "Arrogant, undisciplined" the mediocre call him (...). But when events take a serious turn, the danger becomes pressing, and collective salvation suddenly requires initiative, a taste for risk and steadfastness, then perspectives change and justice shines forth. A sort of groundswell pushes the man of character to the fore.'[20]

Football

On 18 September 1970, Kissinger charged into the office of Bob Haldeman. 'I have to see the president now,' Nixon's national security advisor told the White House chief of staff. 'Why?' asked the man who would be swept up in the Watergate scandal several years later. An incensed Kissinger slammed a file down on the desk and extracted several aerial reconnaissance photographs taken by a U-2 spy plane over Cuba. 'It's a Cuban seaport, Haldeman, and these pictures show the Cubans are building soccer fields.'

Haldeman was nonplussed. Kissinger gesticulated at the images: 'Those soccer fields could mean war, Bob!' Seeing that he still didn't understand, Kissinger spelled it out: 'Cubans play baseball. Russians play soccer.'[1]

That day, Kissinger's love for the beautiful game would enable him to pull off a resounding diplomatic success.

After his meeting with Haldeman, Kissinger was able to convince Nixon to investigate further. The Americans very soon discovered that the Russians were indeed on the ground in Cuba, in direct violation of the agreement that had put an end to the Missile Crisis of 1962. They were providing the Cubans with technical support to build a naval base at Cayo Alcatraz. It was a *casus belli* for the United States. Following very strong pressure on Moscow from the White House, the Soviet leadership were eventually obliged to abandon their project. A major new Cuban crisis had just been avoided.

We have to travel back four decades before that autumn day in 1970 to understand Henry Kissinger's passion for football. It started on his maternal grandfather's farm in Leutershausen, where the young Henry spent his summers. 'I started playing when I was about six,' he would explain later. 'I played goalie for a brief period, then I broke my hand. After that, I played inside-right and midfield. I played until I was 15. I really wasn't very good but I took the game very seriously.'[2]

So seriously did Henry take it that he dreamt up new tactics for his teammates. His chief innovation was to encourage them to pull back and defend, gradually wearing down the opposing team who were rendered incapable of scoring. Of course, it would be a step too far to credit Henry Kissinger with the invention of the famous *catenaccio*. For one thing, this tactical system – popularised by Helenio Herrera when he managed the great Inter Milan in the 1960s – was not purely defensive.

The all-consuming passion of their eldest son for football provoked the consternation of Paula and Louis Kissinger. In an article published in the *Los Angeles Times* in 1986, Kissinger wrote: 'My father despaired of a son who preferred to stand for two hours watching a soccer game rather than sit in comfort at the opera or be protected from the elements in a museum.'[3] Above all, his parents fretted about the risks their son now ran to satisfy his passion.

Once the Nazis took power, Jews were forbidden to set foot in a stadium. But young Henry had become a fervent supporter of SpVgg Fürth, the local club that was the pride of the town, having won the German championship in 1914, 1926 and 1929. Despite risking being beaten up if he were recognised, Henry had taken to sneaking into the stadium to watch his favourite team play, much to his parents' chagrin. 'After '33, going to a soccer match was some adventure for me,' he would later admit.[4]

Yet it was another event that would force him to park his love of football. When he emigrated to Washington Heights with his family in 1938, Henry was quite saddened to discover that nobody he met over there was interested in the game. Put out, the teenager resolved to set his heart on that most American of sports: baseball. The football stars of his childhood gave way to that icon of the New York Yankees, the famous Joe DiMaggio.[5]

This break with football was only temporary, however. A few years later, Kissinger returned to Germany as a solider in the US Army. Once the war was over, he stayed behind in the land of his birth to participate in the denazification campaign. Once again, he could give free rein to his passion, slipping away to watch amateur matches whenever his schedule permitted. He would drive around the countryside at the wheel of his Mercedes – confiscated from a former Nazi – visiting the various football grounds close to his base in the town of Bensheim.

But paradoxically, it was when Kissinger was at the peak of his career that he followed football the closest. As soon as he entered the White House, his staff made it a habit to slip the latest SpVgg Fürth results into his Monday-morning briefing.[6] And it was preferable for their boss's mood – and thus theirs – that these results were good. Above all, Kissinger now received regular invitations from his counterparts to attend matches, notably in Europe and Latin America. As he confided in an interview with Reuters in 2009, this was one of the great pleasures of his life as a diplomat.[7]

On 3 July 1974, on the way back from meeting with the Soviet leadership in Moscow, Kissinger decided to stop in West Germany. The Netherlands, captained by Johan Cruyff, were playing Brazil in one of the most memorable clashes of that World Cup. When Kissinger and his thirty-eight-member security team entered the stadium in Dortmund, the crowd rose as one to give him a standing ovation.[8] Granted, the hero of the evening – during which the *Oranje* schooled the *Seleção* – would forever be the 'Flying Dutchman'. But there is no doubt that Kissinger's ego was lastingly flattered by the acclaim he received that night, particularly since some of his other visits to stadiums would be less well received. In December 1976,

Henry Kissinger

the equally football-mad British foreign secretary, Anthony Crosland, invited his American counterpart to accompany him to Stamford Bridge, the legendary ground of Chelsea F.C. (then in the second division). Shortly before kick-off, Kissinger popped into the dressing room of the home team to say hello. The players, most of whom had no idea who he was, greeted the secretary of state with a mixture of indifference and sarcasm. 'Who's that wanker?' one of them asked.[9]

Such let-downs did not affect Kissinger's love of the game one iota. In fact, he gradually came to realise the extent to which football could be a most useful diplomatic tool.

One morning in May 1973, Kissinger found himself at Zavidovo, the Soviet equivalent of Camp David. He was only the third foreign dignitary to have had the honour of being invited to what was the favourite retreat of the highest political echelons of the USSR. The meeting he was due to have with Leonid Brezhnev, the Soviet leader, was crucial to the success of the summit to be held with Nixon at the White House a few days later. But discussions very quickly became bogged down, whether regarding arms control, nuclear non-proliferation or grain supply, and the exchanges between the two men got progressively frostier. Suddenly, the Soviet leader changed tack: 'I just read a book about Brazilian football.' Aware of Kissinger's love of the game, and himself known to bunk off a Politburo meeting to catch a Dynamo or Lokomotiv Moscow match, Brezhnev embarked on an anecdote about the superlative Brazilian dribbler Garrincha.[10] When negotiations resumed shortly afterwards, they were somewhat more relaxed. A new rapport existed between the two men.

The lesson was not lost on Kissinger. The following year, during a meeting with the steely Polish leader, Edward Gierek, he broke the ice by commenting that Poland would surely have beaten West Germany at the recent World Cup if their free-flowing style had not been hampered by the rain and the atrocious conditions.[11] And it was through teasing Andrei Gromyko about the conflict between East and West through the prism of football that the secretary of state was able to wring a smile from the notoriously dour Soviet minister of foreign affairs.

But there were other world leaders who knew how to play on Kissinger's football mania. In July 1969, the four-day 'Football War' erupted between Honduras and El Salvador, and the Salvadorean foreign minister sought the intercession of Nixon's influential advisor on behalf of his country at any price. To grab his attention, he reminded him that the conflict, the roots of which were long-running, had been sparked by none other than a football match between both countries. 'Anything that arises from soccer, I'm interested in,' Kissinger freely admitted. And he did indeed devote particular attention to this conflict.[12]

Diplomatic game-playing aside, Kissinger also set himself the goal of making soccer popular in his adopted land. This was more than a personal mission; he realised that the rest of the world would always view with a certain suspicion a power that preferred baseball and American football to the beauty and elegance of soccer.

To make his ambition a reality, Kissinger knew that he had to pull off two feats. The first was to attract some of the best footballers on the planet to play in the American championship, a not insignificant challenge given that soccer in the United States was known neither for its excellence nor for the devotion of its fans. Second, he would have to convince FIFA that it was in the interest of the sport for the United States to host the World Cup one day.

To achieve his first goal, Kissinger travelled to São Paulo in early 1975 and invited Pelé to have coffee with him. The Brazilian football legend was in the twilight of his career. He had just announced his international retirement and, lionised the world over, had received some phenomenal offers from Italian

Henry Kissinger

and Spanish clubs. Yet the triple world champion was intent on seeing out his career at his beloved Santos.

But as Pelé would explain in an interview published on 13 May 2016 in *Esquire*, this was before he encountered the persuasive powers of the secretary of state.[13]

At their first meeting, Kissinger got straight to it. 'Listen. You know I'm from the United States, and I'm in politics there. Soccer is coming along there – they're playing it in the schools. Would you like to help us promote soccer in the United States?'[14] Then he explained to Pelé that he would be the ideal figure to give the sport a decisive boost, adding that there was no better club to do this than the New York Cosmos whose owner, Steven Ross, harboured huge ambitions.

A few months later, President Ford welcomed Pelé to the White House. Aware of how little interest the president had in the sport, Kissinger had prepared a briefing note in which he attempted to explain the subtleties of soccer. 'Soccer is a great game to play as well as to watch,' wrote the secretary of state. 'It's easy to learn and, since the object isn't to hide the ball, as in our football, it's easy to follow for the spectator. It doesn't have all those pauses in the action, either.'[15] It isn't certain that Gerald Ford, who'd been a college football star at the University of Michigan, appreciated the manner in which Kissinger gave his opinion of soccer's superiority so frankly.

But Pelé's visit on 28 June 1975 was a diplomatic success. A few weeks later, he donned the Cosmos strip and was soon joined by Franz Beckenbauer. Over the following years, a host of other big-name internationals would make their way Stateside to see out their career in the lucrative North American league.

Kissinger had achieved his first objective, but he knew that bringing the World Cup to the United States would be considerably harder. The man who had successfully conducted myriad thorny negotiations with the most powerful leaders on the planet had underestimated the Machiavellianism and the deviousness of the hardmen of FIFA: its president, the Brazilian João Havelange, and his henchman (and future successor), the Swiss Sepp Blatter.

In 1983, Colombia announced that, because of its disastrous economic situation, it would not be able to hold the 1986 World Cup as planned. Kissinger spied a wonderful opportunity to promote the joint candidature of the United States and Canada as hosts. But in May 1983, after barely considering the joint application, FIFA decided to award the competition to Mexico, following a unanimous vote worthy of a congress of the Chinese Communist Party. The fact that the TV rights were granted to Televisa, the Mexican media empire then run by one of Havelange's close friends, Emilio Azcárraga, was clearly no coincidence.

The United States would have to wait until 1994 to host the World Cup. Kissinger's past failures and the deeply opaque workings of association football's world governing body caused him to quip that 'the politics of FIFA make me nostalgic for the Middle East'.[16]

In 2011, with rumours of corruption swirling around him, Sepp Blatter thought he could muddle through by announcing the establishment of a committee of 'wise men' with the remit of reforming the institution. To give this committee credibility, he declared that Kissinger would sit on it. Kissinger, however, was used to Blatter's craftiness, and had the good sense to ask what this committee's terms of reference would be. The FIFA president never furnished a clear answer, and Kissinger eventually turned the post down. This would prove to be a sage decision given Blatter's fall from grace a couple of years later.

The disillusions he experienced with FIFA did nothing to dent Kissinger's love of football. In September 2012, he returned to the town of his birth to watch his favourite team – now called SpVgg Greuther Fürth – after it was promoted to the Bundesliga.

Henry Kissinger

Above all, the great diplomat remained an avid observer of football, with which he liked to draw parallels with the history of international relations. Talking about the style of play of the *Mannschaft* in an interview with *Sports Illustrated*, Kissinger explained: 'Both the national team and the generals who followed the Schlieffen Plan during World War I paid meticulous attention to detail. But there is a limit to human foresight, and both suffered when, under the pressure of events, they were forced to deal with contingencies that overwhelmed their intricate planning.'[17]

But his expertise extended beyond analysis of the German national squad. In an interview given to the *New York Times* in 2010, Kissinger observed that 'Brazil has played the most beautiful football, while Italy has specialized in breaking the hearts of its opponents.'[18] As for the United States, his team had certainly improved over the years, but 'we don't have a national style that I've been able to figure out. We're a work in progress, just as we are in managing international affairs on a global basis.'[19] The native German reserved his final words for France, however, who 'are always the most elegant team in Europe'.[20]

Glamour

When Henry Kissinger arrived in Washington in January 1969, he was the toast of academia. Few political commentators would have wagered that this portly professor with a strong German accent would also become the darling of the capital's high society.

It was true that Henry had been paying closer attention to his appearance following his divorce in 1964. He had acquired a sun lamp to temper his pallid complexion. His suits and shirts were now made to measure. He had even bought himself a Mercedes coupé, which he drove somewhat erratically. Yet the new national security advisor was still far from a fashion icon. Everything about his physique and bearing recalled the academic he had been.

But the American capital was desperate to shrug off the torpor that had weighed on it since the end of the Kennedy years. Washington high society was on the lookout for new figures who could provide a little glamour. Such candidates in the Nixon administration were few and far between. Like the president, most of his advisors and cabinet members disdained the media and the Washington set. Which was fortunate for Kissinger, who had discerned that, in 1970s America, power and celebrity were common bedfellows. A man who acquired celebrity would enjoy an aura that would boost his influence. Kissinger also realised the importance of networking. He excelled in forging close connections with the capital's foremost journalists, notably the Alsop brothers and the political commentator Tom Braden.

*

Henry Kissinger

So it was that during the first two years of the Nixon presidency, Kissinger buckled down to becoming the new golden boy of Washington society. Every evening would see him grace yet another of the fine homes in Georgetown. At dinners, which invariably ended at 10 p.m., prominent senators rubbed shoulders with media barons, influential journalists and powerful lawyers and lobbyists, along with a sprinkling of ambassadors and millionaires. It was at these gatherings that Kissinger would deploy all his charm.

His keen mind, his sparkling wit and the many secrets he would blithely share delighted the other guests. Kissinger wanted to be liked at any cost and he had found an extremely receptive milieu. In particular, he had all the right ingredients to be adopted by a city that lived and breathed politics: power, sharp intuition and a charisma methodically honed through contact with the great and the good. He aspired to be the person whom everyone noticed when he walked into a room.

Kissinger's prestige really soared, however, when his secret trip to China, and the negotiations he was undertaking in Paris with the North Vietnamese, became public knowledge in 1971. His reputation now stretched far beyond the cosy Georgetown salons. Everyone wanted to be seen alongside the man who made the cover of *Newsweek* below the headline 'Super K'.[1] Kissinger was developing a multifarious network, which would take him all the way to Hollywood.

Before entering the White House, Kissinger travelled to California to take part in several conferences at the RAND Corporation, a prestigious think tank based in Santa Monica. Privately, though, he had always been drawn to the glitz of the City of Angels, and his growing popularity now opened every door, so why not take advantage of it? Courted by the most powerful producers in the American film business, he used his regular visits to La Casa Pacifica – President Nixon's estate in San Clemente – to drop by Hollywood whenever he could.

Glamour

Kissinger liked being snapped alongside stars of the silver screen. One evening, when Kirk Douglas and his wife Ann were passing through Washington, he invited them to have dinner along with Tom Braden and his wife. Arriving late at Rive Gauche, an upscale and fashionable French bistro, Henry found Douglas and the other guests already settled at an alcove table towards the back of the restaurant. Much to Douglas's protestations, an insistent Kissinger demanded that they be seated where everyone could see them. All evening long, a procession of fellow diners pestered them for autographs and handshakes. Kirk Douglas's exasperation was equalled only by Kissinger's glee.[2] More than any movie star, he sought the light.

When in Hollywood, Kissinger also liked spending a not inconsiderable portion of his free time in the company of young female leads and actresses – many of whom were known more for their looks than for their acting talents. Already an unexpected celebrity, Kissinger would become an even more improbable sex symbol.

A 1972 survey of *Playboy* bunnies – those young waitresses employed at *Playboy* Clubs and sometimes called upon to feature in the magazine as Playmates – revealed that Kissinger was their number-one choice for an amorous tryst. This caused many to wonder how a man who never exercised, and of whom the masseur at San Clemente observed that 'he did not have a muscle in his body',[3] enjoyed such success with women. The master of American diplomacy famously replied: 'Power is the great aphrodisiac.'[4]

Kissinger carefully nurtured his playboy reputation. It was he who slipped Sally Quinn, society columnist at the *Washington Post*, the expression 'secret swinger' with which he would now be labelled.[5] Rumour also had it that, not content with being photographed in the company of ravishing young women, he would sometimes contact the paparazzi himself ahead of a night on the town, to let them know where to find him.

*

Henry Kissinger

On 21 November 1972, while deep in negotiations with the North Vietnamese leadership in Paris, he invited a former sweetheart, Jan Cushing, to lunch at Chez Tante Louise, a restaurant located close to the US embassy. Kissinger, whose trip to the French capital was no longer a secret, was pursued by a horde of journalists. With lunch over, and the world's press gathered outside, the restaurant's maître d'hôtel suggested that Kissinger leave discreetly by a side door to escape the paparazzi. 'No,' replied the national security advisor with a smile, before getting up and strolling proudly out of the front door. But instead of stepping into the official car waiting for him, he walked up and down the street beside his stunning companion. The next day, the photograph of Kissinger with this 'mysterious young blonde' made front pages around the world.

Henry liked nothing more than talking about his new reputation. When the famous NBC journalist Barbara Walters asked him how it felt to be 'a new kind of sex symbol in Washington', his gaze suddenly sparkled. The man who dreamt of himself as a twentieth-century Metternich enthusiastically replied: 'I love it,' adding, with a twinkle: 'Now when I bore people, they think it's their fault.'[6]

In September 1971, the fashion trade journal *Women's Wear Daily* published a pen portrait of Kissinger, under the headline: 'I wonder who's kissing now'. The article begins: 'Henry Kissinger, sex symbol of the Nixon Administration',[7] later quoting one of his friends: 'Henry likes to believe that although he's a serious Germanic scholar, he's really a frivolous playboy, that he's Metternich, the Papillion [sic], light, gay and 18th Century.'[8]

Yet it's true that Kissinger appeared to enjoy a succession of conquests. Samantha Eggar, Candice Bergen and Liv Ullmann were just some of the actresses who were seen out and about with him in the society pages. One evening, he was snapped flirting with the actress Jill St John at Trader Vic's, a tiki bar at the Los Angeles Hilton. The next evening, at a society dinner in Hollywood, his companion, the superb dancer and actress Ann Miller, who was well aware of Henry's reputation, teased him for such public displays of frivolity 'while our boys in Vietnam are getting their heads shot off'. The mood suddenly darkened. 'Miss Miller,' he said, no longer calling her Ann, 'you don't know anything about me. I was miserable in a marriage for most of my life. I never had any fun. Now is my chance to enjoy myself. When this administration goes out, I'm going back to being a professor. But while I'm in the position I'm in, I'm damn well going to make it count.'[9]

Actresses, dancers, singers, journalists – all the women seen on the arm of the most improbable playboy of the twentieth century agreed on one thing: Henry stood out for his kindness and his patience.[10] They could call him late at night and he would always take the time to listen to their worries and to comfort them. They all admitted, too, that their relationship with Henry remained purely platonic. During the moments they spent together, he liked to touch their hands and stroke their hair. But once dinner was over, he drove them home – a dozen Secret Service agents in tow – and went back to work.

At a party in Washington in 1969, Kissinger was introduced to Barbara Howar, a fixture of the capital's social scene. Sitting on a couch with her, he confided that he and Nixon were flying to Midway the next day to discuss troop withdrawals from Vietnam with President Thiệu. 'If you bring about a withdrawal from Vietnam,' she told him with passion, 'you can call me and do whatever you want with me.' Kissinger took her hand and, looking her straight in the eye, replied: 'Dinner will be sufficient.'[11] In an interview given to the Italian journalist Oriana Fallaci in 1972, Kissinger summarised his outlook less than elegantly: 'For me women are only a diversion, a hobby. Nobody devotes too much time with his hobbies.'[12]

What he left unsaid was that it was preferable that his

conquests did not see the inside of his apartment. Despite being one of the most powerful men in the world, Kissinger's one-bedroom home near Rock Creek Park looked like a slovenly student's pad. There were no paintings on the walls, nor any other decorative element, just a few photos of himself in the company of foreign heads of state. In the bedroom, two single beds stood next to each other. Above one of them, the master of American diplomacy would hang his freshly washed underwear, socks and shirts. Once a week, a cleaning lady came by to restore a semblance of order.

Kissinger's playboy reputation amused his colleagues at the White House and cemented his aura with some of them. Even Nixon joked about it. One afternoon, as he waved off his advisor, who was leaving La Casa Pacifica – dubbed the 'Western White House' – to head up to Hollywood for the evening, the president grinned at Kissinger and said: 'Don't do anything I wouldn't do tonight, Henry.'[13]

In those dark days, when the spectre of Vietnam hung heavy over a divided nation with little to celebrate, the White House PR team were not averse to the press going to town on Kissinger's love life. A little lightness and glamour could do the White House no harm.

Yet Nixon took increasing umbrage at his advisor's fame. He was also aware of Kissinger's tendency, at these society gatherings, to let slip details about him that were often less than favourable. So he decided to hit Henry where he knew it would hurt. Not long after his arrival in the administration, Kissinger had made a deal with the White House social secretary, Lucy Winchester. She agreed to ensure that he would systematically be seated next to the most beautiful women at state dinners. But one morning in 1971, the day after an official dinner, Kissinger burst into Winchester's office in a rage: 'Lucy! You sat me next to a ninety-eight-year-old crone!'[14] But Lucy Winchester had had no say in the matter. A few days earlier, she had received the following memo, on the orders of the president himself: 'In seating at State Dinners, the President feels that Henry should not always be put next to the most glamorous woman present. He should be put by an intelligent and interesting dinner partner and we should shift from the practice of putting him next to the best looking one. It's starting to cause unfavorable talk that serves no useful purpose.'[15]

Despite such minor disagreements, the approach of his fiftieth birthday saw Kissinger's stardom attain new heights. A 1973 Gallup poll voted him the person whom Americans most admired. That same year, he was named 'the greatest person in the world today' by a sizeable majority of Miss Universe contestants. A member of Congress, Jonathan Bingham, even proposed an amendment to the Constitution that would allow a citizen born outside the United States to stand for president. The newspapers were full of fawning articles, one of which was headlined: 'Henry Kissinger, the virtuoso, at 50'.[16]

The party held to celebrate his fiftieth birthday was a reflection of Kissinger's celebrity and power. It was hosted at New York's Colony Club – a private establishment for women from very good families – on Park Avenue. The guest list was testimony to the strength and diversity of Henry's network, and included Nelson Rockefeller and eminent members of the Nixon administration, as well as the owner of the *Washington Post* (Katharine Graham) and star journalists such as Mike Wallace, David Frost and Walter Cronkite.

Less than a year later, though, Kissinger's days as a playboy bachelor would come to an end when Nancy Maginnes, a stunning woman eleven years his junior, finally agreed to marry him.

Henry and Nancy first met in 1964 when they were both working for Nelson Rockefeller. Kissinger immediately fell under the spell of this bright and ambitious young woman. He proposed to her then, but she felt it was far too soon and turned him down. But they continued to see each other nevertheless.

After Kissinger entered the White House in 1969, Nancy would come to visit him in Washington nearly every weekend. Only Henry's closest friends, such as the Alsops and the Bradens, were aware of Nancy's place in his life.

For the refugee desperate for recognition that Henry Kissinger had always been, Nancy Maginnes ticked all the boxes. Scion of a wealthy East Coast family, this discreetly elegant woman with perfect manners fulfilled his desire for social ascension. Nancy was more than comfortable in high society and had an eclectic network stretching well beyond the political sphere. And unlike the starlets in whose company Kissinger was frequently seen in the press, Nancy hated the limelight and lent him a much-needed touch of respectability. Kissinger may have been secretary of state and considered one of the most powerful men in the world, but his friends were still surprised to hear him say, on more than one occasion: 'Can you believe that she's a member of the Colony Club and wants to marry me?'[17]

The wedding day was postponed six times, because of Kissinger's excessively busy schedule, but Henry and Nancy were finally married in a small ceremony on 30 March 1974 following a meeting at the White House with Moshe Dayan. Shortly afterwards, the newlyweds jetted off on Nelson Rockefeller's private plane to Acapulco for their honeymoon. There, protected by Kissinger's Secret Service detail and twenty Mexican policemen, and pursued by forty-odd paparazzi scrutinising their every move, Nancy realised that her taste for discretion would be sorely tested.

When Kissinger left office in January 1977 and returned to live in New York, he felt it necessary to retain the symbolic attributes of power. Bereft of the protection of the Secret Service, he hired five bodyguards to work for him round the clock. He

Glamour

travelled only by private jet; commercial airlines would have been an insult to a man of his standing. The Kissingers split their time between their Manhattan apartment overlooking the East River and a property they acquired in Kent, Connecticut – a location prized by New York high society and much more discreet than the Hamptons. Here, Henry and Nancy would spend their weekends and the whole of August. Each year, they would spend the festive season at Oscar de la Renta's stylish villa in the Dominican Republic and fly to Acapulco in February.

Such a lifestyle supposes a considerable income. This would initially derive from the several volumes of bestselling memoirs penned by Henry, dealing with his years at the White House. But he also entered the business world, which was prepared to pay top dollar for his unique address book and keen geopolitical analyses. He joined the boards of a string of companies, some of which paid extremely handsomely – as did speeches and appearances. In 1982, Henry launched Kissinger Associates, a geopolitical consultancy whose clients included some of the biggest companies in the world and which would allow him to retain a prominent platform.

Little by little, Henry Kissinger became part of the jet set. Figures from the worlds of politics, the media, cinema and fashion graced the dinners hosted by the Kissingers at their Manhattan apartment or their Connecticut estate. The annual general assembly of the United Nations would see a string of foreign heads of state visit him in New York each September. Henry also attended the meetings of such prestigious yet select clubs as the Bohemian or the Bilderberg Group. His birthday parties were opportunities to show off the scope and power of his network. The Clintons, media magnate Rupert Murdoch, theatre and film director Peter Glenville and the founder of Atlantic Records, Ahmet Ertegün, were just some of the personalities in Kissinger's entourage.

Aged fifteen, Henry had arrived in Washington Heights in far northwest Manhattan, penniless and not speaking English.

Henry Kissinger

He was to become a pillar of New York high society, his calendar full months in advance. He continued to travel around the world and succeeded in finding a balance between media appearances, writing new books and his business activities. He liked the mix of glamour, power and money, of which he now had no shortage. Yet something was lacking in this life he had built for himself: the adrenalin of his years in power. He no longer had the feeling of writing history and changing the course of events. Neither his constantly busy schedule nor his luxury lifestyle could mask this reality. He sensed this relatively quickly and tried to return to public life. In 1980, he pulled all sorts of strings in an attempt to be named secretary of state under Reagan. But Reagan had never liked Kissinger and opposed the idea. Next, Kissinger thought to leverage his immense popularity to become senator of the State of New York. But he very quickly realised that his skin was not thick enough to withstand the personal attacks that come with a life in politics. He also knew that the controversies regarding his past actions could come back to bite him. So he gave up on his dreams of returning to centre stage.

Henry Kissinger may not have experienced the heady feeling of power again, but he was able to conquer new territories after leaving office. The man who had made his mark in academia and then at the heights of world diplomacy became a star of the business and media world, and a figure of the jet set. At the root of this incredible career was the exceptional network he had begun building from his first years at Harvard. There are indeed few people who have had the talent and perseverance to forge, nurture and exploit such a diverse and cosmopolitan network.

Harvard

Our current era has seen many young leaders take office. Often in their thirties or forties, they give the impression that the race to reach the highest echelons of power has become a sprint. They relentlessly seek the limelight; products of a culture of immediacy in which public relations is all. But many of them are just shooting stars, destined to fade away as fast as they appeared in the political and media firmament. Such people may be gifted in leveraging the fleeting mood of a nation to attain power, but their lack of intellectual depth or emotional intelligence prevents them from retaining it for very long. Their terms of office are either insignificant or marked by shallow gambles – such as that made by David Cameron with the Brexit referendum – which deal lasting damage to their nations. Few manage to achieve re-election or merit more than a footnote in the history books.

The contrast with Henry Kissinger is striking. He entered the White House a few weeks shy of his forty-sixth birthday but would turn fifty before becoming the leading US diplomat. The man who took the oath of office on 22 September 1973 as the fifty-sixth secretary of state of the United States had already experienced trials and tragedies aplenty.

The young Henry had known hatred, exile and war. His adult life as a father and Harvard professor brought him emotional and intellectual fulfilment. Since adolescence, he had constantly been working; reading and delving into the works of great authors and deepening his knowledge of history in order to understand the world around him better.

Much has been said and written about Kissinger's Machiavellianism and nous for scheming. His political astuteness and ability to surround himself with influential patrons are undeniable. Nevertheless, they would have been little help to Kissinger had he not already put in the requisite work. Scheming can get you a top job, but the exercise of power is a merciless judge of those who are not up to it.

The twenty years that Henry Kissinger spent at Harvard therefore played a crucial role. It was here that he acquired many of the qualities that later enabled him to stamp a mark on history out of all proportion to what would have resulted from the simple fulfilment of his duties.

When Henry Kissinger first walked across Harvard Yard in autumn 1947, the campus was an exciting place to be. In the lecture halls, young students, barely out of high school, sat alongside men who had fought in the war, thanks to the 1944 G.I. Bill, which enabled so many demobbed soldiers to continue their studies. Driven by a thirst for life that only the experience of war's horror can confer, they brought a unique spirit to the university.

While an 'iron curtain' had descended across the European continent (as Churchill put it), and the Cold War was ramping up, Harvard was beginning to assume the role that it would hold from then on.[1] The Second World War sealed the end of a global order dominated by Europe. But unlike the 1920s, when isolationism still reigned supreme in Washington, the United States was now ready to assume its role as the leading world power. Harvard would become *the* institution to train the future élites of the 'free world'.

For Henry Kissinger, then aged twenty-four, his first weeks on campus were a brutal transition. Just a few months earlier he had been the undisputed master of a region of Germany that he was responsible for denazifying; now, he suddenly found himself a nobody among the 1,598 first-year students. From a lavish life in a superb villa in the heart of the German countryside, he had to share a modest room with two other students, both fellow Jewish army veterans.

Harvard

*

In this new environment, Henry devoted himself to his studies, body and soul. He would rise at seven in the morning to study in the library, not returning to his room before late afternoon, whereupon he would ensconce himself in a deep armchair and work his way through borrowed books, griping whenever the authors evinced erroneous reasoning. He read the *New York Times* and the *Boston Globe* every day, though not the editorials, considering that he should form his own opinions.

There was no time for distractions in this ascetic schedule. Despite Henry's taste for sport, he was not a member of any team and never set foot in the stadium. He didn't go to parties either and gave the impression of being an introverted young man. Many of his fellows thought he was arrogant, because of his perpetual air of serious aloofness. He was yet to make humour the precious ally that would allow him to win over so many people years later.

Academically, his marks were top-notch and a world of possibilities opened up to him. As comfortable in the humanities as he was in the sciences, for a few months Henry flirted with specialising in chemistry. But he soon realised that his aspirations leant primarily towards political philosophy and world affairs. He would also make the acquaintance of someone who would prove decisive in his choice of career path.

When Henry attended a lecture by William Yandell Elliott for the first time, he realised that he was in the presence of a living Harvard legend. A lover of poetry and literature from his youngest days, Elliott had fought in Europe in the First World War, after which he stayed to continue his studies at the Sorbonne and then at Oxford, where he excelled and developed a taste for philosophy and history. Hired by Harvard, he made the department of political science his fiefdom, where he was admired as much as he was feared. Ferociously anti-communist and hugely erudite, Elliott had garnered a reputation as a talent spotter, taking under his wing such figures as McGeorge Bundy (national security advisor to presidents Kennedy and Johnson) and the future Canadian prime minister Pierre Trudeau.[2] Hailing from a very poor family in small-town Tennessee, there was a certain magnetism about this flamboyant, quixotic professor, which could only attract Kissinger.

Although young Henry's marks were sufficient to allow him to ask Elliott to be his tutor, their first tutorial made him realise that he would need to do something really special to grab the professor's attention. Elliott barely looked at his student, before dismissing him after a few minutes, having given him a reading list of twenty-five titles and instructing him not to return until he had read them all and written an essay comparing Emmanuel Kant's *Critique of Pure Reason* with his *Critique of Practical Reason*.

Far from being discouraged, Henry saw this as an opportunity to prove his worth to the man he wanted to be his new mentor. For several weeks, he worked in the library all the hours that God gave him. Then one day, at dawn, he slipped his essay under Elliott's office door. In the early afternoon, while he was finally taking some time to rest in his room, Henry received a message summoning him to his professor's office immediately. Their second tutorial would mark the start of a relationship that, just like those forged with Fritz Kraemer and Nelson Rockefeller, would have a major influence on Kissinger's personal development.

Upon reading Henry's essay, Elliott immediately sensed a 'feeling for political philosophy' and that 'he was not blind to the epic nature of history'.[3] He decided to make Henry one of his protégés. In the course of their long Sunday walks, Elliott was insistent about the importance of thinking freely and independently. The bond that gradually developed between the two men became so strong that, despite certain future disagreements – notably over the policy of Détente – Kissinger would pay the following tribute upon his master's retirement in 1963: 'Whatever I have achieved, I owe importantly to his inspiration.'[4]

Kissinger worked flat-out to attain his goals. In 1950, he submitted his undergraduate dissertation, whose title – 'The meaning of history'[5] – sums up all its ambition. In it, he stated his conviction that free will prevails over all kinds of determinism. This 383-page dissertation, in which he undertook a comparative analysis of the works of the philosophers Emmanuel Kant, Oswald Spengler and Arnold J. Toynbee, earned him top marks. But, taken aback by the unprecedented length of Henry's dissertation, his supervisors instituted the so-called 'Kissinger rule', stating that, from that day forth, dissertations could not exceed one-third of the length of that submitted by the latter. Thus, Henry Kissinger entered into Harvard legend for the first time.

With this first stage out of the way, Kissinger, after much vacillating, decided to pursue a doctorate within the Department of Government. He was well aware that he was embarking on a highly competitive path, the eventual goal of which was to be appointed professor at Harvard. But Kissinger knew that to achieve this holy grail, dreamt of by entire generations of doctoral students, Elliott's benevolent patronage would not suffice. He therefore made sure to nurture good relations with every influential professor at the university.

Very quickly, though, Henry realised that his taste for scheming and manoeuvring would never be sated within the world of academia. This is one of the reasons he established, with Elliott's support, the Harvard International Seminar in 1951. Kissinger was convinced that the most famous university in the United States was a magnificent venue for bringing together young American and European leaders to share their views of the major geopolitical issues and partake of the best that the American intellectual scene had to offer. It was American soft power par excellence.

At a personal level, the International Seminar gave Kissinger the opportunity to forge links with those building the Europe of tomorrow. This was how he met future French president Valéry Giscard d'Estaing, future Belgian prime minister Leo Tindemans and, as the geographical scope of the programme expanded, future Japanese prime minister Yasuhiro Nakasone, future Turkish prime minister Bülent Ecevit and future Israeli foreign affairs minister Yigal Allon.

A year after the inaugural International Seminar, Kissinger also decided to found a quarterly journal on world affairs. Named *Confluence*, it had a print run of just over 5,000 copies. Over the course of the somewhat austerely designed journal's six-year existence, it never had much commercial success. But this mattered little to Kissinger. *Confluence* brought him into the orbit of such prestigious contributors as the historian and philosopher Hannah Arendt, the theoretician of international relations Hans Morgenthau, and the economist John Kenneth Galbraith. The young doctoral student understood that *Confluence* was a wonderful means of contacting the great and the good. There was not a statesman, a journalist or an intellectual who would not be flattered to be asked to pen an article for a journal published by Harvard University.

The International Seminar and *Confluence* enabled Kissinger to boost his profile and to understand how the powerful progressed. He learned how to treat them and to charm them. They, meanwhile, were struck by the intelligence and the energy of this young, ambitious man.

Meanwhile, Henry was also making headway with his thesis, the subject of which was the way in which two major European figures of the nineteenth century, Prince Klemens von Metternich and Viscount Castlereagh, laid the foundations of a lasting balance of power on the European continent following Napoleon's defeat. This allowed Henry to expand on the themes of

Realpolitik and conservatism so dear to him. He also found it to be a propitious conduit for several important messages he wished to convey regarding his views on the balance of powers in the context of the Cold War. His work was also nourished by the challenging discussions and debates he continually had with the other students.

Although Harvard has always had the reputation of being a mecca for the finest minds, this has rarely been as justified as it was during this period. Alongside Kissinger, we find such students as Stanley Hoffmann, Judith N. Shklar and Samuel Huntington, who would become major figures in American academic and intellectual circles. But it was with a brilliant student of Polish origin named Zbigniew Brzeziński that an intense rivalry developed. The doctoral jousting between Nixon's future national security advisor and the man who would hold this post under President Carter presaged their combative relations as statesmen.

As one might imagine, the competition to be named professor at Harvard was fiercer than ever. When Kissinger submitted his thesis in 1954,[6] he nevertheless hoped that the combination of his academic work, the projects he was pursuing and the patronage he now enjoyed would open the way for him. So it was with supreme confidence that he asked McGeorge Bundy, then the youngest dean of the Faculty of Arts and Sciences and a true star on campus, if it would be possible to get tenure in four or five years' time instead of – for those lucky enough to receive it – the usual seven or eight. Henry was gobsmacked when Bundy, with a condescending smirk, answered him in the negative.

Kissinger refused to be downhearted. If Harvard wouldn't open its doors to him, he would just have to prove his worth elsewhere. So he packed his bags for New York, where he divided his time between the Council on Foreign Relations and his consulting services for Nelson Rockefeller, whose close collaborator he would soon become. And he began to write his first book, *Nuclear Weapons and Foreign Policy*,[7] in which he espoused a strategy of 'flexible response' as opposed to the strategy of 'massive retaliation' then in vogue with the Eisenhower administration. Published in 1957, the book quickly established his name beyond academia.

When Henry returned to Harvard that autumn and presented himself to McGeorge Bundy, it was with a newly burnished profile. Even though some professors considered that it was not appropriate for a future colleague to express himself on subjects they judged to be more political than purely academic, Bundy was now persuaded that Henry deserved his place on the teaching staff in the Department of Government. In 1959, Kissinger was named associate professor at the same time as Stanley Hoffmann. Three years later, he was made a full professor. Woody Allen riffed on this in his film *Annie Hall*, declaring, in the character of Alvy Singer: 'Hey, Harvard makes mistakes too! Kissinger taught there!'[8]

But for Henry, the days of counting pennies were over. As was the era of driving around in an old second-hand Dodge and living in a modest apartment in Arlington Heights with Anneliese (Ann) Fleischer, whom he had married in 1949. He and his family, which now included Elizabeth, born in 1959, and David, born three years later, were able to move into a comfortable house in Cambridge, very close to the university.

Above all, Kissinger was now free to devote more time to the subjects that really interested him. During these years, he furthered his research in numerous geopolitical fields, with a particular interest in questions of nuclear deterrence. He also continued to expand his network of American and international decisionmakers, while keeping abreast of the work of his Harvard fellows. And he finally found time to write a long paper on Bismarck – a figure who had always fascinated him – which was published in the academic journal *Daedalus* in 1968.[9]

Harvard

In his application to be a doctoral student at Harvard, Kissinger had written: 'I hope upon receiving my graduate degree to become affiliated with a university in a teaching or research capacity, though I have not excluded the possibility of entering government service.'[10] What he hadn't anticipated was that his second ambition would be considerably nourished by the first. Harvard was much more than a stage in his life. It was a unique place where he gained the qualities that would allow him to become a statesman.

Helsinki

2 July 1975. A stifling heat grips Washington. In the Oval Office, Gerald Ford paces back and forth. Should he agree to receive Aleksandr Solzhenitsyn at the White House?

A little earlier that day, two senators, Jesse Helms and Strom Thurmond – as influential as they were conservative – had asked the Counselor to the President, Jack Marsh, to set up a meeting with the most famous Soviet dissident as quickly as possible.[1] Ford was hesitant.

Granted, he was well aware that the winner of the 1970 Nobel Prize in Literature was considered a real hero by a sizeable chunk of the American elite and the media. From left to right of the political chessboard, there were many for whom Solzhenitsyn was the figurehead of the fight against communism. Arrested on 12 February 1974, stripped of his nationality and deported from the USSR the next day, the author of *The Gulag Archipelago* eventually found refuge in Vermont after spending several months in Europe.

But the geopolitical environment rendered the holding of such a meeting immensely delicate. Ford was due to fly to Helsinki a few days later to attend the final stage of the Conference on Security and Co-operation in Europe, which had been established two years previously by the United States, the USSR, Canada and every European country except for Albania. Presented as the apogee of Détente, its final act, according to Kissinger, was supposed to consign the logic of blocs to the past.

In this context, the secretary of state's recommendation to his president was clear: Ford must not receive Solzhenitsyn under any circumstances. Such a meeting would be an affront to the Soviet leadership, notably Brezhnev, and would risk collapsing the entire policy of Détente that Kissinger had been patiently building over the past few years.[2]

Kissinger's recommendation was all the stronger given that Solzhenitsyn no longer even bothered to hide his aversion to the policy pursued by the Ford administration. Invited to address the AFL-CIO (the American Federation of Labor and Congress of Industrial Organizations – the largest federation of unions in the United States) on 30 June, the Soviet dissident had launched a merciless attack on the negotiations under way in the Finnish capital. In stark contrast to the strategy espoused by Kissinger, Solzhenitsyn advocated total confrontation with Moscow. He called upon the United States to tirelessly fight communism wherever it existed in the world, including within the borders of the Soviet Union. 'Interfere more and more,' he preached to an enthusiastic audience. 'Interfere as much as you can. We beg you to come and interfere.'[3]

When he was informed of these words, Kissinger flew into a rage.

His irritation with Solzhenitsyn had been brewing for some time. The previous year, the Ford administration had tried to persuade Congress to confer 'most favoured nation status' on the USSR, a gesture that Kissinger believed would strengthen the trust between Moscow and Washington, at little cost. He also wanted to take advantage of what the international lawyer Samuel Pisar, a specialist in East–West relations, described as 'the soothing power of economic and cultural exchanges between the Americans and the Russians'.[4] But in light of the emotive reactions to the translation and publication of *The Gulag Archipelago* in the United States around that time, Congress put its foot down. This was a major defeat for a man now accustomed to success.

In that summer of 1975, Kissinger would not countenance

Solzhenitsyn blocking his path again. But he could rely on Gerald Ford, though, who had not the slightest desire to spend several hours being lectured by a man who, as even the most fervent admirers acknowledged, was more amply blessed with intellect than with charm. The White House therefore decided not to grant the Soviet dissident a meeting.

It was predictable that this decision would spark heated debate among the public. And the appalling communication on the matter would turn the situation into a political disaster for the US government.

The White House press secretary, Ron Nessen, initially gave the explanation that President Ford 'was simply unable to fit Solzhenitsyn into his schedule'. This garnered dubitative, even sarcastic, reactions from a sizeable proportion of the press. Shifting strategy, Nessen explained the next day that 'for image reasons, the President does like to have some substance in his meetings', adding that 'it is not clear what he would gain by a meeting with Solzhenitsyn'.[5]

Across Washington there was consternation. It was an open secret that the incumbent of the White House liked receiving beauty contest winners and famous sportsmen. A few days earlier, he had posed beside Pelé, all smiles.[6] It was a bit rich to suggest that the author of *One Day in the Life of Ivan Denisovich* had less substance than these various other guests.

In the face of ballooning polemic, Ford and Kissinger realised that they needed to backpedal as fast as could be. The White House announced that Solzhenitsyn was invited to meet the president whenever he desired. But it was too late. Angered by Ford's prevarications, the Soviet dissident declined the invitation, making the withering comment: 'Nobody needs symbolic meetings.'[7]

The split between Solzhenitsyn and the Ford administration was definitive.

*

Henry Kissinger

The long-distance duel between Solzhenitsyn and Kissinger took on a new dimension on 15 July 1975, when the two men, speaking 900 miles apart, laid out two irreconcilable visions of American foreign policy.

Standing before Congress, the Soviet dissident made a concerted attack on the policy of Détente in which he saw the creeping 'spirit of Munich'. In his eyes, the Helsinki conference marked nothing less than 'the funeral of Eastern Europe'. Employing his metaphorical verve, the Russian poet went on to describe it as 'an amicable agreement of diplomatic shovels [that] will inter in a common grave bodies that are still breathing'.[8]

These words could only find favourable echo on both the Republican and the Democrat benches. In a gesture of defiance to the Ford administration, and Kissinger in particular, the members of Congress rose to their feet and gave Solzhenitsyn a standing ovation.

At the same moment, in Minneapolis, in the heart of the Midwest, Henry Kissinger was preparing to give one of the most important speeches of his career.

It is paradoxical that despite his taste for secrecy in the art of diplomacy, Kissinger, more than any other American statesman, sought to publicly explain the motivations of his foreign policy decisions. Driven by a desire to persuade even his most fervent adversaries, and convinced that an understanding of the major geopolitical issues should not remain the monopoly of a minority, he considered that it behoved him as secretary of state to educate as to the reasoning behind his actions.

It was deep in the heart of America – in regions far removed from the large urban areas of the East Coast where the political and intellectual elites resided – that Kissinger travelled to explain the aims and the twists and turns of American foreign policy to ordinary citizens. Despite his excessively busy schedule, he would spend hours writing and rewriting his speeches, sometimes working late into the night. This man, whom many commentators described as the very embodiment of elitism, had faith in his fellow citizens' ability to comprehend the subtleties of his actions.

On that 15 July, Kissinger knew that his audience feared that Helsinki would be a new Yalta. The American people suspected their leaders of being prepared yet again to sacrifice the citizens of Eastern Europe on the altar of peace with Moscow.

In his speech titled 'The moral foundations of foreign policy', Kissinger recalled the motivations of Détente, emphasising that, in an age of thermonuclear threat, statesmen had no other choice but 'to seek a more productive and stable relationship [between the Eastern and Western blocs] despite the basic antagonism of our values'. Moreover, Kissinger in no way denied the *Realpolitik* that guided his actions: 'We no longer live in so simple a world (...) Consequently our own choices are more difficult and complex.' On a geopolitical chessboard 'where power remains the ultimate arbiter', the policy of Détente was therefore one that allowed the 'furthering of America's interests'.[9]

His brilliant speech earned Kissinger the applause of a crowd won over by the charm and intelligence of this refugee of German origin who personified American achievement. But opposition to the Helsinki conference remained extremely strong in the rest of the country.

With the 1976 presidential election fast approaching, foreign policy became a domestic policy issue, as Democrats and Republicans alike skirmished ahead of the coming battle. Within the Republican party, the fiercest criticisms of Détente came from the man whom many saw as the new rising star of the conservative right: Ronald Reagan.

The governor of California had never liked Kissinger. The gulf between the former B-movie actor and the Harvard professor was simply too vast.

Reagan, who was gearing up to challenge Ford in the Republican primaries, could not condemn the Helsinki conference harshly enough. He saw it as a humiliation for the 'free world'.

On 25 July 1975, a few days before the signing of the Helsinki Final Act, Reagan declared at a press conference: 'I am against it, and I think all Americans should be against it.'[10]

Kissinger and Ford never succeeded in touching the heart of America and creating sufficient buy-in for Détente. Reagan, however, understood, in that summer of 1975, that American society was now more disposed to moral crusades. Behind the ideological disagreement opposing Kissinger and Reagan lay something crueller for the secretary of state: for the first time in his career, he symbolised the past.

It was therefore against an extremely fraught domestic backdrop that President Ford boarded a plane to Europe on 26 July. When he stepped up to the lectern in Finlandia Hall five days later, he knew that the whole world was listening. In his speech, he did his utmost to allay the concerns of those who thought that Washington was preparing to abandon Eastern Europe to its fate. As he finished speaking, he turned to Brezhnev and, looking the Soviet leader straight in the eye, said: 'History will judge this conference not by what we say today, but what we do tomorrow; not by the promises we make but by the promises we keep.'[11]

These words would prove prophetic.

While the Soviet leadership focused on the formal recognition of the spheres of influence inherited from the Second World War, they made the mistake of neglecting the human rights provisions of Helsinki. In his own speech, Brezhnev even thought they could be ignored, declaring that 'no one should try to dictate to other peoples on the basis of foreign policy considerations of one kind or another the manner in which they ought to manage their internal affairs. It is only the people of each given State and no one else, who have the sovereign right to resolve their internal affairs and establish their internal laws.'[12] It was a grievous error.

In the months following the signing of the Final Act, dozens of so-called 'Helsinki' groups were formed across the countries of the Eastern Bloc. In Czechoslovakia, the playwright Václav Havel led Charter 77, while the Polish union leader Lech Wałęsa launched the Solidarność movement in the Gdansk shipyards. All demanded that the Communist authorities respect the clauses of the Helsinki Accords as regards fundamental freedoms and human rights. Less than fifteen years later, Havel and Wałęsa took office following democratic elections.

What most observers and political leaders failed to see, both in Moscow and in Washington, was that Helsinki would be the catalyst for major political upheavals in Eastern Europe. As Gerald Ford would explain many years later: 'Henry [Kissinger] and I were accused of trying to freeze Yalta. But what Helsinki really brought about was pressure for human rights, and that has got to be one ingredient for what happened in 1989.'[13] As aware as Ford was of the damage this episode inflicted on his political career, he would nevertheless state towards the end of his life that he was 'prouder than ever to have signed the Helsinki accords'.[14]

In an American democracy already subject to the diktats of short-termism, public opinion, however, could not grasp the benefits and the pertinence of an accord that would take several years to bear fruit. The strident blows inflicted by Reagan and the conservative wing of the Republican party would lay the groundwork for Jimmy Carter's victory in 1976, which brought to a close Kissinger's career as a statesman. He would never hold power again.

Ever since entering the White House in 1969, Kissinger had been admired like no other leader of his generation. For several years, he had been lauded for his policies, some of which would prove to be failures. He had been awarded the Nobel Peace Prize in 1973 for his diplomatic efforts in Vietnam, even though the country would take many long years to leave war behind. It is an irony of history that Kissinger's end as a statesman would be triggered by one of his greatest achievements.

Henry Kissinger

In 1975, the wheel had turned. Kissinger's brand of European realism had no place in a nation aspiring to reconnect with an idealism that would give it a clearer conscience. The very same people who had lacked sufficient superlatives to praise the brilliant diplomat now saw him as a manipulator devoid of any morals. From then on, no matter that the Finnish capital was the scene of one of the greatest American victories of the Cold War, Helsinki would forever embody Henry Kissinger's downfall.

Humour

For many years, Henry Kissinger seemed to lack a sense of humour. As a student at Harvard, he never so much as ventured the slightest witticism. Even the flicker of a smile was a rare occurrence. His pompous manner and flattery of the academic staff elicited much mockery on the part of his peers, however. If a smile was cracked in his vicinity, it was usually at Kissinger's expense.

Yet, just a few years earlier, the young Henry had noticed how precious an ally humour could be. Having recently joined the army, he found himself the target of antisemitic slurs by some of his young, unsophisticated comrades – more from ignorance than actual malice. Yet Kissinger managed to gain their respect through a subtle mix of self-deprecation and irony.

It would be a long while before he drew the lessons of this experience. It was only when he entered the race to become a Harvard professor that he understood he could no longer rely on his intelligence alone. In the eyes of those around him, he saw the sparks of envy at his burgeoning success. His arrogance aroused distrust. His vanity provoked scorn.

Henry realised then that only self-deprecation could make the most annoying aspects of his personality acceptable to others. So he decided to employ humour in the furtherance of his ambitions. Underpinned by the weight of his intelligence, it would become a fearsome weapon.

Humour did not come at all naturally to Kissinger. Its acquisition was not accidental, but the result of meticulous work to create a tool to seduce and persuade in pursuit of his limitless ambition.

Kissinger began honing his sense of humour among his students. In his class on the principles of international relations, he took real pleasure in indulging in oratorical sparring. While many of his students were in favour of unilateral nuclear disarmament on the part of the United States – a view then popular with a section of the American left – he tried to persuade them otherwise, as much through quips as through his erudition. Even his most diehard opponents were not insensitive to his charming humour.

To those who considered him pretentious, Kissinger would respond by sending up his own successes. Although his first book had received effusive praise[1] and found itself on the *New York Times* bestseller list, he remarked to one of his friends: 'I am sure that it is the most unread best-seller since Toynbee.'[2]

It was the same when it came to mitigating his perceived arrogance. To a journalist who questioned him on his influence in the White House, he began by replying quite seriously: 'I have been called indispensable and a miracle worker.' Then, after a beat, he added, with a twinkle in his eye: 'I know, because I remember every word I say.'[3]

While his sycophantic manner was a subject of ridicule at Harvard, his toadying to Nixon opened him up to much more acerbic criticisms. Well aware of this, Kissinger turned it to his advantage. There was an anecdote he liked to recount of how Nixon came back from a weekend at Camp David one time and proudly announced: 'I shot 126.' To which Kissinger slickly replied: 'Your golf game is improving, Mr President,' only for Nixon to growl: 'I was bowling, Henry!'[4]

As thin-skinned as he was, Kissinger tried, at least in public, to lampoon the enmities, even hatred, aimed at him. His rivalry with the secretary of state, William Rogers, was an open secret, so he preferred to joke about it. 'Everyone in the State Department is trying to knife me in the back except for Bill Bundy [one of the key architects of the Vietnam War]. He is still enough of a gentleman to knife me in the chest.'[5]

The humour that allowed Kissinger to parry certain attacks also became a tool to attract and retain the best collaborators.

Kissinger was not one of those high officials who fear surrounding themselves with top talent. He was imbued with sufficient confidence in his intellectual qualities to appreciate being stimulated, even contradicted, by the rising stars of American diplomacy. But, known for his epic rages and his cutting remarks, he was also aware that he needed to spread some levity around if he wished to avoid seeing his protégés quit one after another.

At the White House, at the State Department and then at Kissinger Associates, he tried to employ humour to inject a little humanity into relations with his colleagues. For example, having just moved into a vast office at the White House, he joked to his staff that his office was now so huge that by the time he had stomped across the room and flung open the door to give someone a dressing down, he had sometimes forgotten what had riled him in the first place.[6]

People who spent time around the master of American diplomacy also noticed that he was more receptive to remarks that were made to him with a touch of humour. In January 1971, his relationship with Nixon was going through a rather turbulent patch. Kissinger even threatened to resign. As he paced around his office, fulminating, the president's speechwriter, William Safire, listened to him patiently, his calmness only serving to make Kissinger even more apoplectic. 'You guys think I'm kidding when I say this, but I'll resign! I don't have to put up with this!' Safire replied coolly: 'If you quit, Henry, you'll never get a phone call from a beautiful woman again. The secret of your attraction is your proximity to power.' Kissinger quickly relaxed: 'You're right about that, Safire, it would be a tremendous sacrifice.'[7]

Against all expectations, the chubby professor with the pale complexion had, since his divorce in 1964, morphed into a dandy who was more than receptive to the charms of the fairer sex. Despite lacking a 'Tarzan physique', as one of his conquests put it,[8] Henry took great pains to maintain his reputation as a ladies' man once he entered the White House.

But Kissinger was aware of the limits of his mantra that 'power is the great aphrodisiac'. He knew he would have to deploy every ounce of his wit if he wanted to seduce Washington's most beautiful women. And deploy it he did. The celebrity pages of magazines printed many pen portraits in which a host of women praised his 'quick wit'.[9] His former peers at Harvard must have been flabbergasted.

In employing humour for seductive purposes, Kissinger was nevertheless merely following in the footsteps of his role model, Metternich. The great Austrian diplomat, known for his many romantic conquests, is described by Kissinger in his undergraduate dissertation as having a level of conversation that was 'brilliant but without ultimate seriousness'.[10]

Beyond successful womanising, which flattered his ego and delighted readers of the society pages, Kissinger strove to make humour a trump card in his diplomatic hand. He wanted to charm world leaders with his witticisms too. Yet he would quickly realise that big political beasts are not as easy to win over as the Hollywood starlets with whom he enjoyed being snapped by the paparazzi.

When he met Hafez al-Assad for the first time, Kissinger thought he could win him over with a joke. Knowing that the Syrian leader was learning English, he offered his help. 'You'll be the first Arab leader to speak English with a German accent,' he told Assad with a twinkle, only to be met with a long and increasingly awkward silence. Kissinger then tried to wring a smile from the Lion of Damascus with a few risqué remarks regarding his own female conquests – a subject of conversation he knew some Arab leaders relished. Assad's icy gaze told him that this was a dead end.[11]

Humour

*

Respected by his peers for his intelligence and his strategic vision, Kissinger remained the object of ridicule in chanceries the world over. Many found amusing his propensity to make contradicting arguments depending on who he was talking to. Nowhere was this more apparent than in the Middle East, where his 'shuttle diplomacy' involved him playing the intermediary between the Arab and Israeli leaders.

In Cairo, Ismail Fahmi, the Egyptian foreign minister, was always much more circumspect than his president, Anwar Sadat, regarding Kissinger's sincerity. But it was above all the Israeli leadership, notably Shimon Peres and Yitzhak Rabin, who mistrusted the American diplomatic maestro the most, as shown by a joke then popular among the Israeli elite:

> Kissinger decides to play matchmaker and informs a poor peasant that he has found the perfect wife for his son. 'But I never meddle in my son's affairs,' says the peasant.
>
> 'Ah, but the girl is the daughter of Lord Rothschild,' says Kissinger.
>
> 'Well, in that case ...'
>
> Kissinger then goes to Lord Rothschild. 'I have the perfect husband for your daughter,' he says.
>
> 'But she's too young,' Lord Rothschild protests.
>
> 'Ah, but the boy is a vice president of the World Bank.'
>
> 'Well, in that case ...'
>
> Kissinger then goes to the president of the World Bank, saying, 'Have *I* got a vice president for *you!*'
>
> 'But we don't need another one.'
>
> 'Ah,' says Kissinger, 'but he is the son-in-law of Lord Rothschild.'

Kissinger also used humour to mask his own fragilities, such as his complex relationship with his Jewishness. He would often joke about it instead of talking more seriously. Invited to the bar

Henry Kissinger

mitzvah of the son of Israel's ambassador to Washington, the secretary of state was asked by one of the other guests if the ceremony was very different from his own, which had taken place four decades before in Fürth. With utmost gravity, Kissinger replied: 'Ribbentrop did not come to my bar mitzvah.'[12]

The way in which Kissinger was able to make humour one of his aces, in both his private and public life, reflects the political and diplomatic genius of the man. But it also raises a more fundamental question regarding the evolution of our society. At a time when moral censoriousness is back in vogue, would Kissinger's brand of acerbic humour be tolerated today? As freedom of expression is fettered a little more each day, on the pretext of catering to everyone's own hypersensitivities, would the kind of withering remarks wielded by Kissinger provoke a public backlash? Kissinger reached the highest spheres of American diplomacy at a time when humour was still seen as a positive quality, where a witty remark would boost a person's reputation in most people's eyes. We can only look at this period with a certain nostalgia.

Indefensible?

In an era that likes nothing more than reviling that which was once venerated, Kissinger is increasingly viewed as a 'criminal', an 'imperialist' and a 'murderer'. At a time when many journalists and commentators feel as if they must don the robes of a modern-day public accuser in order to exist, Henry Kissinger has become a prime target. That they judge his past actions in the light of current moral criteria, omitting the thousand and one contextual complexities of his time, matters little to them. It all serves to fuel the self-righteous censoriousness that now serves as morality to vast swathes of our Western societies.

For years now, a multitude of books and articles have discharged a flood of hatred and calumny on Henry Kissinger. Playing the role of public accuser in chief, the British journalist Christopher Hitchens readily considered Kissinger to be no better than the greatest mass murderers and most bloodthirsty dictators of the twentieth century. For Hitchens, whose views have been widely disseminated by a mass media keen to discredit a man they had long praised to the skies, Kissinger was guilty of nothing less than 'crimes against humanity'. Hitchens depicts an amoral, cynical creature, not a master of diplomacy.[1]

It behoves us, therefore, to explore the exact details of the charges levelled at Henry Kissinger. First, it is striking to note that the attacks on him come as much from the right of the political spectrum as from the left. Indeed, it is sometimes for radically opposing reasons that his reputation is dragged through the mud.

For one section of the right, Kissinger has only ever been a 'wimp', an 'intellectual' much too accommodating of America's enemies. In the 1970s, Reagan vilified the policy of Détente, which he saw as the illustration of Kissinger's weakness in the face of the Kremlin. At a press conference he gave in Orlando on 4 March 1976, the then governor of California stated: 'Henry Kissinger's stewardship of United States foreign policy has coincided precisely with the loss of United States military supremacy.'[2] At the Republican National Convention in Kansas City several months later, he added: 'Under Kissinger and Ford this nation has become No. 2 in military power in a world where it is dangerous – if not fatal – to be second best.'[3]

The neoconservative wing of the Republican Party has always felt that Kissinger was only importing a European-style *Realpolitik* that ran contrary to American values. Because he never believed that the United States had a supposed messianic vocation, Kissinger refused to engage America in crusades aiming to impose democracy across the world, a stance that led neoconservatives to accuse him of denying and betraying the soul of America. Deep down, though, it was Kissinger's European heritage that a section of the right could never accept. The criticisms of his policy masked a continual questioning of the American identity of this former German Jewish refugee.

Accused in his own country of being insufficiently American, abroad Kissinger was the target of criticisms that were often rooted in an anti-Americanism. This was among the more painful of the many paradoxes that dotted this man's life.

However, it was from liberals and the left that the harshest attacks against Henry Kissinger's personality and actions came. For many, the former secretary of state was a war criminal whose terrible crimes knew no bounds, whether moral or geographic. The principal accusations can be summed up as follows.

First, Kissinger was accused of having shamefully prolonged the Vietnam War for electoral reasons. Although he had come to the conclusion, as early as 1966, that the United States would not come out of this conflict as victors, he supposedly sabotaged the peace negotiations that the Johnson administration was pursuing with the North and South Vietnamese in Paris.[4] Kissinger, who had contacts in the negotiation team but was also advising the Republican camp, supposedly did this with the aim of weakening the Democrats, so laying the groundwork for a Nixon victory in November 1968. Between Nixon's election and the American withdrawal in January 1973, more than 20,000 American soldiers and more than half a million Vietnamese lost their lives.

For many of his critics, Kissinger's name is also tragically associated with the fate of Cambodia. Although this country had proclaimed its neutrality in the conflict ravaging its Vietnamese neighbour, Kissinger is accused of having been the chief architect of a secret bombing campaign that killed more than 600,000 people and precipitated the tiny kingdom's plunge into a decade of atrocities. From 18 March 1969 to August 1973, American B-52 bombers dropped a greater tonnage of bombs on Cambodia than the Allies had dropped in total during the whole of the Second World War.[5] In the view of Hitchens, Noam Chomsky and many others, these bombings, which the Nixon administration wished to keep under tight wraps to avoid Congress's critical gaze, created the conditions for Pol Pot's barbaric Khmer Rouge regime to seize power.[6]

Bangladesh was another place where Kissinger was accused of having been the silent accomplice to the atrocities perpetrated by his Pakistani ally.[7] In 1971, after Bangladesh (hitherto the Pakistani province of East Pakistan) declared independence, Islamabad launched a military campaign of unbelievable violence. The Pakistani army used rape as a systematic weapon of war, accompanied by massacres and summary executions. By late 1971, half a million Bangladeshis had been killed, more than 200,000 women had been raped and 10 million civilians had fled to neighbouring India as refugees. Despite the alarming telegrams sent by American diplomats in the country, including the heroic Archer Blood, consul general to Dhaka, Kissinger closed his eyes to the crimes committed by his Pakistani ally.[8] Worse, he ensured that those in the State Department who tried to call for a policy of support of the Bangladeshis were dismissed or sidelined. The master of American diplomacy considered Pakistan to be a key ally, particularly given that the regime of General Yahya Khan was playing a highly secret role as intermediary between Washington and Beijing.

Kissinger was also heavily criticised for maintaining a guilty silence in the face of the abuses perpetrated several years later by one of the closest allies of the United States, Indonesia.

It all started in Portugal in April 1974 when the Carnation Revolution triggered the fall of the Salazarist dictatorship. In the Portuguese colony of East Timor, democracy was flowering. Three main political parties emerged, including the Revolutionary Front for an Independent East Timor (Fretilin for short), which was of Marxist persuasion. After several weeks of tensions and violence between these various movements, Fretilin established its domination of the island and unilaterally declared the independence of East Timor, which was recognised by Lisbon on 28 November 1975.

But things moved very fast. On 6 December, Kissinger and Ford met with the Indonesian president, Suharto, in Jakarta. The dictator, who feared the establishment of a Communist regime at his door and the destabilisation of the entire Indonesian archipelago, announced his intention to annex his Timorese neighbour. Unsettled by the recent tumble of the Vietnamese domino and keen on preserving the alliance with the largest non-communist nation in Southeast Asia, Kissinger did nothing to dissuade Suharto and the Indonesian generals from pursuing their plans.[9]

The next day, the Indonesian army launched Operation Lotus. By spring 1976, there were over 30,000 Indonesian troops in East Timor committing terrible atrocities. The violent

Indefensible?

occupation would last twenty-five years and see the death of close to 100,000 Timorese. And although the repression undertaken by the Indonesian army was in violation of the military aid agreements between Jakarta and Washington, Kissinger did his utmost to ensure that the United States maintained its support for Suharto's regime. Again, he shut down any dissident voices within the State Department.[10]

Over the past decades, many journalists and historians have also focused on Henry Kissinger's actions in Latin America. Researchers have attempted to shed complete light on Kissinger's links with the Argentinean dictatorship led by General Videla. Kissinger was accused of having shown great passivity, both when he was in power and in the years that followed, about a regime responsible for the death of over 30,000 people and the exile of millions of Argentineans.[11]

But it was the role played by the former secretary of state in the tragic events that took place in Chile that has drawn the fiercest criticisms.

From the early 1960s, presidents Kennedy and Johnson had pursued policies aiming to prevent the socialist Salvador Allende coming to power. Defeated at the ballot box in 1964, Allende was nevertheless democratically elected to the presidency of Chile in September 1970. The spectre of the Cold War, the links forged by Allende with Fidel Castro and tensions within Chile led Kissinger to conclude that this country was no longer merely 'a dagger pointing straight at the heart of Antarctica'; the threat was increasingly aimed at America.

In this context, the man then preparing to be secretary of state is accused of having orchestrated and covered up a series of clandestine actions resulting in the coup against Salvador Allende on 11 September 1973 and the establishment of a military dictatorship under General Augusto Pinochet.[12] Several decades later, declassified files of the 1975 Senate Church Committee, which investigated abuses by US intelligence services,

57

revealed that Richard Helms, the director of the CIA at the time, had admitted that some of his contacts had been actively involved in the carrying out and covering up of serious human rights abuses.[13]

Despite Pinochet's military junta torturing tens of thousands of civilians and disappearing several thousand more, Kissinger made sure that the public condemnations expressed by the United States never translated into an actual weakening of relations between the Chilean dictatorship and Washington.[14]

But it was in Europe that Kissinger was accused of having committed some of his gravest misdeeds. One of the chief accusations against him has to do with his attitude during the coup d'état in Cyprus on 15 July 1974. According to his detractors, Kissinger knew about the intention of Greece's Regime of the Colonels to topple the president of the Republic of Cyprus, Archbishop Makarios III, but did nothing to dissuade Athens from getting rid of the man he saw as 'the Fidel Castro of the eastern Mediterranean'.[15] Nor would he express any opposition to the many human rights violations and exactions committed by the Greek junta who sought to unify Cyprus with Greece by force. On the contrary, he once more lent his weight to the preservation of good relations with a country whose ports were essential to the US Sixth Fleet.[16]

Reading such an unremitting indictment, even the most gifted lawyer might be tempted to refuse to take on the defendant's case. Yet one can't help thinking of Pope Urban VIII's alleged response to being told of the death of Richelieu – words that Kissinger himself quoted (oh, the irony) in *Diplomacy*: 'If there is a God, the Cardinal de Richelieu will have much to answer for. If not ... well, he had a successful life.'

Without wishing to diminish Henry Kissinger's responsibility or assume the role of judge as regards his actions in office, we should bear in mind the context in which they occurred. It would indeed be a mistake to forget the uncertainties, the fears and the hopes that filled the leaders of the West and their

Indefensible?

citizens. Every situation is different, of course, but there was one thing that loomed constantly over every decision taken by Henry Kissinger: the shadow of the Cold War.

For Kissinger, who had personally suffered so much from the barbaric Nazi regime, the ultimate moral goal was to preserve the stability of the world. In the nuclear age this meant reducing as much as possible the risk of a direct confrontation between the two superpowers while also avoiding the disintegration of the 'free world' in the face of the Soviet menace. Kissinger knew that to achieve this objective, he had no choice but to tread a delicate path as regards both bilateral relations between Washington and Moscow and the various conflicts that might break out across the world.[17]

Kissinger was convinced that the Soviet system would crumble progressively as soon as its leaders were no longer able to extend their sphere of influence or invoke imminent foreign threats to justify the oppression of the peoples under their boot. It was this reasoning that led Kissinger to develop and implement the policy of Détente – a policy that earned him fierce opprobrium, both from hawks calling for direct confrontation with Moscow and from isolationists and doves who wished to cease the political, military and ideological struggle with the Kremlin. But in the long term it was indeed Détente that brought the USSR to its collapse and enabled the United States to win the Cold War.

Ronald Reagan and George H.W. Bush had the fortune to be in the White House when it came to harvesting the fruits of this victory, but it was the result of the strategy dreamt up and applied by Kissinger. And it was this very strategy that justified so many of the controversial decisions for which the former secretary of state is so widely castigated today.

Take Vietnam. In 1965, Henry Kissinger travelled there at the invitation of Henry Cabot Lodge Jr, the US ambassador to South Vietnam.[18] Exasperated by his university colleagues who peremptorily analysed and judged the war in Vietnam from atop their ivory towers, the young Harvard professor wanted to take the measure of the reality on the ground. What he saw there convinced him that an American military victory was impossible. However, he also realised that an immediate withdrawal by the United States was equally impossible.

For Kissinger, the crucial question was that of the United States' credibility.[19] Credibility regarding not only rival powers – first and foremost the USSR – but also allied countries. If Washington suddenly abandoned its South Vietnamese ally, he was sure that many governments across the world would no longer trust America's word. Some might even be tempted to swap the shelter of the US military umbrella for the Soviet one, thus weakening the whole system of alliances so patiently constructed by the United States since the end of the Second World War. For Nixon and his national security advisor, this was out of the question.

But the two men also shared the opinion that, in the absence of a military victory, they could still tip the balance of power in favour of their South Vietnamese ally before the last GI left the Indochinese Peninsula. Nevertheless, Kissinger knew that such a policy would require time and that it supposed a *gradual* withdrawal of US forces, rather than a sudden one. It was this that guided the Nixon administration, as much in Vietnam as in Laos and Cambodia.

Regarding Cambodia, Kissinger deemed that the Kingdom's neutrality was only theoretical. The Vietcong were using this country as a rear base to launch numerous deadly attacks against American and South Vietnamese troops. For Kissinger, the bombing campaign on Cambodia, undertaken with the agreement of General Lon Nol's government, was not a moral issue, but a tactical imperative, which, according to his logic, should have ensured an orderly and safer withdrawal of American troops.

As Kissinger explained in an interview he gave to *Die Zeit*: 'The fact is that we were bombing North Vietnamese troops that had invaded Cambodia, that were killing many Americans from these sanctuaries, and we were doing it with the acquiescence of the Cambodian government, which never once protested against it, and which, indeed, encouraged us to do it.'[20] To those who consider the American bombings morally comparable with crimes perpetrated by the Khmer Rouge, he pointed out: 'In the six years of the war, not 10 per cent of the people had been killed in Cambodia than had been killed in one year of Communist rule.'[21] As costly as the American military operations in Indochina were in human lives, Cambodia paid a much higher price owing to the genocide carried out by the Khmer Rouge from 1975 to 1979. Estimates vary, but it is considered that between 1.5 million and 3 million Cambodians lost their lives, out of a total population of 8 million.[22]

Although Kissinger admitted (at a Congressional hearing in 1975)[23] that the American bombings deeply destabilised Cambodia, it would be reductive to attribute the takeover of the country by Pol Pot and his accomplices to these operations alone. It would be even more intellectually dishonest to see those bombings as furnishing the reasons for the insanity of the Khmer Rouge's campaign of mass slaughter. As numerous historians have shown, many factors explain the coming to power of the Khmer Rouge in a Cambodian society already heavily weakened by the operations carried out on its territory by North Vietnam.[24] Rather than blame Kissinger for crimes committed by those he was in fact attempting to fight, it would be more pertinent to remember that Kampuchea was supported and armed by the People's Republic of China from the start.

Henry Kissinger's stances on East Timor, Bangladesh and Chile also have their roots in the primacy he gave to a *Realpolitik* that sought, above all, to preserve American diplomacy's room for manoeuvre in shifting geopolitical circumstances that were sometimes extremely difficult for the United States to navigate.[25]

Henry Kissinger

In 1975, the Kremlin seemed to be gaining ever more ground in the face of its American foe. South Vietnam's capitulation on 30 April marked a major setback for Washington. With the entire American nation weakened and divided by a dirty war that had become a collective national trauma, the alliance with Indonesia seemed more precious than ever to the Washington strategists. Suharto's regime increasingly appeared as the ultimate rampart against the spread of communism through Southeast Asia. When the Jakarta strongman spoke to President Ford and his secretary of state of his intention to invade the tiny Timorese nation, Kissinger's calculation was a simple one. East Timor's fate, as tragic as it might be, weighed much less in the balance than the need not to offend or weaken his Indonesian ally.

We should also note that the stance taken by the Ford administration was far from an isolated one. A similar policy was pursued by Jimmy Carter, despite the crimes committed by the Indonesian troops on the Timorese population. Under the Carter administration, huge quantities of military materiel were delivered to Indonesia. In 1979, Australia would even formally recognise the Indonesian annexation of East Timor, while France and the United Kingdom would lend discreet yet genuine diplomatic support to the Suharto regime.[26]

If the importance of America's alliance with Jakarta explains Kissinger's attitude to East Timor, the value he placed on another alliance – that between Washington and Islamabad – was the source of his extremely controversial policy in Bangladesh.

Nixon and Kissinger had understood that if they wanted to open up new vistas of action to American diplomacy, they would have to be the architects of a new global balance of powers. But this meant returning China to the geopolitical chessboard. As the pair saw it, the move to a tripolar order should offer the United States new avenues of action and weaken the Kremlin by forcing a latent breach between Moscow and Beijing. But

Indefensible?

Kissinger knew that to achieve this ambition he needed the aid of the Pakistani regime, which had very close links with the Chinese leadership. During the Bangladesh War of Independence and then the third India–Pakistan War, strategic considerations once again took precedence over any moral qualms.

When it comes to Chile, the precise role played by Kissinger in the coup that took place on 11 September 1973 remains the subject of much debate among historians. What is incontestable, however, is that Kissinger's policy, under both the presidency of Salvador Allende and the dictatorship of Augusto Pinochet, was guided by his obsession with seeing any geopolitical upheaval through the prism of Soviet–American rivalry. For him, as for his predecessors at the head of the State Department, tolerating a pro-Marxist government in Chile was a risk that the United States could not afford. This conviction was reinforced by the attitude of Allende who, once elected, forged close links with Fidel Castro. In later interviews, Kissinger himself admitted that it seemed necessary to prevent Salvador Allende taking or staying in office – at any cost. Because of 'the perils to our interests and to the Western Hemisphere' of letting Chile fall into the lap of the communists, he felt that it was legitimate for the United States to act 'in the grey area between diplomacy and military intervention',[27] as the Soviet Union so often did.

Whatever judgement one may make regarding the actions of Henry Kissinger, it is undeniable that he sought constantly to root his diplomacy in a long-term vision that left little room for the diktats of emotion. Like George Kennan before him, Kissinger had understood that, when it comes to the geopolitical chessboard, those who let themselves be guided by their feelings and their emotions always end up in checkmate.

But at a time when the foreign policy of our Western democracies seems to fluctuate according to public opinion, or even the vagaries of social media, Kissinger's cold and rational realism upsets many sensibilities. As prompt as such people are to criticise and vilify the former secretary of state, they rarely ask themselves a fundamental question: what would have happened otherwise?

It is impossible to furnish an exact answer, but this does not mean that the question can be ignored. The simple fact of asking it reminds us that diplomacy almost always supposes choosing between imperfect moves on a geopolitical chessboard where the line between good and evil is often blurred. Neither high principles nor ideologies can ever be the sole guide.

In our interdependent world, where every decision has its quid pro quos and repercussions that are sometimes hard to anticipate, Kissinger had the courage to *make* choices, as questionable as they may have been, rather than avoiding them. In the Indochinese Peninsula, in Chile, in Cyprus, in East Timor and in Bangladesh, he took policy decisions that he was aware would cause suffering and misfortune for some. But he took those decisions because he felt they were necessary to preserve a global stability that he knew to be fragile and that he deemed to be a higher moral goal. For better or for worse, it seems impossible today to imagine the leader of a great democracy taking and standing by similar decisions to those taken by Kissinger when he was in office.

This assessment should not, however, obscure the fact that Henry Kissinger made some serious errors of analysis for which the United States and its allies paid a heavy price.

Bangladesh was one. Kissinger was wrong to view the India–Pakistan conflict purely through the framing of the Cold War. In rejecting other perspectives and in being blinded by his and Nixon's personal hatred for the Indian Prime Minister, Indira Gandhi, he was unable to foresee how the conflict might play out. He believed that India had got involved in this war with the aim of breaking apart the two territories of Pakistan, and that China would come to the aid of its ally in Islamabad.[28] None of these predictions proved correct. Beijing never interfered in the conflict and, on 16 December 1971, India proposed a ceasefire to its rival, Pakistan, which Pakistan was only too happy to accept. New Delhi didn't even seek to profit from its military success by taking back control of certain territories it claimed in Kashmir.

As a consequence of Kissinger's erroneous assessments, Washington underestimated the atrocities carried out by its Pakistani ally and treated it with a culpable benevolence. All the way through, the Nixon administration remained in denial of both the humanitarian and military reality of the situation, refusing to see that Islamabad was heading straight for a humiliating defeat. The total failure of American diplomacy in Bangladesh deeply damaged relations between Washington and New Delhi and would diminish American influence in the Indian subcontinent for a very long time.

It was not only Kissinger's actions that were so controversial. His attitude to them also drew anger and resentment.

The fact that the former secretary of state devoted not a single line to East Timor in his memoirs raised eyebrows, despite there being more than a thousand pages covering the period from 1974 to 1976.[29] And although he was asked many times about the details of his meeting with Suharto on 6 December 1975, Kissinger systematically denied that the Indonesian leader ever revealed his intention to invade his neighbour. As in so many other cases, it was not until the official files were declassified by the American authorities that some light was shed on the web of lies Kissinger wove to cover himself after leaving office.

Kissinger's paranoia, his ambiguous relationship with the truth and the arrogance he often showed have done much to shape the legend of a man for whom no dishonourable act was too great to slake his thirst for power. Yet although Kissinger's genius lay in his ability to craft a long-term foreign policy that would withstand the whims of public opinion, the fact that his behaviour left him wide open to attacks by those who considered him to be amoral was a major mistake. In the kingdom of puritanical hypocrisy that the United States can be, to boast insolently of your amorality places you on shaky political ground very fast.

Any lawyer agreeing to defend Henry Kissinger would doubtless find him to be a difficult client to help. Many of his policies and actions raise questions, not to mention legitimate criticisms. Above all, the man's apparent amorality would not endear him to a jury deliberating on his case. But the fact remains that the accusations against him reveal a deeper question on the state of our Western societies, particularly in Europe.

As we painfully move on from being the agents of history to being mere bystanders to the world as it evolves around us, we no longer wish to make the difficult decisions incumbent on a great power. Our societies demand immediate gains that are often incompatible with long-term strategy. Even more revealing is our tendency to shun statesmen and stateswomen. Their courage and their sense of responsibility endlessly remind us that reality imposes a permanent tension between our moral values and our interests.

Now, more than ever, Europe needs leaders who are also strategists if it wishes to pull itself out of the pit into which it has sunk. Such individuals need to be capable of developing new analytical frameworks to conceive diplomacy over the long term and understand the strengths and weaknesses of their adversaries. They also need to have the character and talent to put this diplomacy into practice and bear the weight of responsibilities that will accompany their actions.

Despite his faults, his mistakes and his personal weaknesses, Kissinger knew how to do both. Whatever the controversies that will always be associated with his actions, this duality is what made him one of the great figures of the twentieth century.

Jewishness

Henry Kissinger always had a complex relationship with his Jewish identity. Born Heinz Alfred Kissinger into a family who made sure to pass this heritage on to him, it informed his intellectual and spiritual outlook. But his Jewishness was also synonymous with suffering, persecution and humiliation, particularly as he entered his teenage years. Once he became an American, Henry gave the impression of disconnecting from it, or even sometimes hiding it.

Could he accomplish his ambitions without rejecting his heritage? Would he ever be seen as an American and not merely as an American Jew? These questions seem to have tortured him all his life. They are also where we might find the source of some of his biggest decisions, in both his personal life and in office.

Kissinger's relationship with his Jewishness cannot be understood without considering the antisemitism of which he was the victim during his childhood. When Hitler came to power in 1933, an entire world collapsed for young Heinz. He could no longer stroll the streets of Fürth without fearing a beating or a bevy of insults. Life's little pleasures were suddenly barred to him. He could no longer go to watch his favourite football team or take a dip in the river close to his maternal grandparents' farm. His father, whom he admired more than anyone in the world, was relieved of his teaching post as if he were some sort of scoundrel. Above all, Heinz witnessed how the attitudes of people around him changed. The neighbours, once so friendly and kind, now turned their noses up at his family. His few non-Jewish friends refused to play with him. At the age of fifteen, he was forced to flee the country of his birth for one reason alone: being Jewish.

In the orthodox Jewish neighbourhood of New York's Washington Heights where his parents set up their new home, Henry was constantly brought back to his Jewishness. At high school, his classmates were Jews. On weekends, he joined activities organised by Jewish youth movements. In his family's building, all the neighbours were Jewish. Even his first love, whom he would marry, was Jewish.

Yet Kissinger already knew that he didn't want to shutter himself in this environment. He yearned to assimilate into the country that had welcomed his kith and kin. His nostalgia for Germany was gradually displaced by his love for the United States of America, a land where he could walk tall and where he didn't feel obliged to cross the street whenever a group approached him. The young man wanted to be American first, Jewish second. To be an American meant shedding an identity that Kissinger would shun throughout his life: that of a victim.

The spiritual aspect of Judaism was what Kissinger would step away from first. Although he continued to accompany his beloved father to synagogue, it was only so as not to upset him. Having lost thirteen members of his family in the Shoah, something had broken in Henry's faith. It calls to mind the reflections of the Romanian Jewish writer Elie Wiesel. During his time imprisoned in the camps, Wiesel was forced by the SS to watch the hanging of an eleven-year-old boy who took more than half an hour to die. He later described the experience in his memoir *Night*:

> And we were forced to look at him at close range. He was still alive when I passed him. His tongue was still red, his eyes not yet extinguished. Behind me, I heard the same man asking:
> 'For God's sake, where is God?'

Jewishness

And from within me, I heard a voice answer:

'Where He is? This is where – hanging here from this gallows ...'

That night, the soup tasted of corpses.[1]

As paradoxical as it may seem, it was the Second World War that enabled Henry to free himself of his Jewish identity. Kissinger's army service enshrined his 'Americanness' first and foremost. At boot camp, at Lafayette College and then on the European front, his ethnic background was secondary. He appreciated the company of his Midwestern comrades in arms as well as those from the Rust Belt. Through them, he discovered and grew to love an America far removed from Washington Heights.

Back in his native Germany, he refused to let his Jewish identity get the better of his duties as an American soldier. He made it a rule never to express any sign of hatred or desire for vengeance against German civilians, many of whom he knew full well had unreservedly supported the antisemitic policies of the Nazi regime. Through this discipline, which he also enforced on his comrades, Kissinger wanted to show that he would never let anyone or anything reductively define him by his simple Jewishness.

With each career step that he climbed to the highest offices of state, Kissinger left a little more of his Jewishness behind. He ceased any religious practice. His second wife, Nancy Maginnes, was from a rich Protestant East Coast family. But it was above all in the exercise of power that he would adopt attitudes and positions that provoked the incomprehension of his fellow Jews, who saw in him the embodiment of the 'conflicted Jew'.

The bullying and humiliations of his youth imbued Kissinger with an irrepressible desire to please. In particular, he was keen to curry favour with the powerful and be accepted, even loved, by those who it might be supposed would hate him for his ethnicity alone. In this respect, it is striking to note the efforts he made to win over leaders, such as Hafez al-Assad and King

Henry Kissinger

Faisal of Saudi Arabia, whose antisemitism was a secret for no one. But it was with the man he would serve for five years in the White House, Richard Nixon, that this aspect of his character would come into clearest focus; Kissinger's sycophancy often edged out any attachment to his ethnic origins.

Nixon had an extremely complex relationship to Jews. He was the first president to appoint a Jewish secretary of state. And in the White House he surrounded himself with numerous Jewish advisors, including his White House Counsel, Leonard Garment, his economic advisor, Arthur Burns, and his speechwriter, William Safire. Safire would in fact highlight the president's great admiration for Jewish figures such as the late-nineteenth-century British prime minister Benjamin Disraeli, the Supreme Court judges Louis Brandeis and Felix Frankfurter, and the writer Herman Wouk.[2]

Yet Nixon was an antisemite, as the recordings of his private conversations in the White House revealed without a shred of ambiguity. Almost daily, he would launch into hate-filled diatribes against the Jews. 'Washington is full of Jews,' 'Most Jews are disloyal,' 'Goddamn his Jewish soul!' are the sort of things his staff would get used to hearing.[3] He habitually saw conspiracies everywhere, and at times when his paranoia got the better of him, his antisemitism would ramp up to fever pitch. During these moments he would complain to White House chief of staff H.R. Haldeman that the Jews controlled the government and were actively engaged in sabotaging his presidency. Long after he left office, Kissinger would himself recognise the president's antisemitism and try to explain it thus: 'Nixon shared many of the prejudices of the uprooted, California lower-middle class from which he had come.'[4]

Nixon's antisemitism also came through in the relationship he developed with his national security advisor. The pair would meet at least five or six times a day. Indeed, Nixon confessed that Kissinger was 'the man that has the greatest influence on me'.[5] But he took a perverse pleasure in making antisemitic remarks to Kissinger's face, then waiting to see his reaction. Kissinger would nervously wiggle his feet, but otherwise he never contradicted the president. Even when Nixon called American Jews 'traitors' and doubted their bravery in Vietnam, Kissinger's answer was always a deafening silence.[6]

When one of his colleagues asked him why he never said anything, Kissinger answered that to do so would be counter-productive and futile. He would lose the president's trust and be excluded from his inner circle, meaning that he would no longer be able to put forward his point of view on key political issues. What's more, explained Kissinger, Nixon's antisemitic rantings did not worry him unduly given that, most of the time, they carried no political implications.[7] It was also easier for him to close his ears because he knew how complex a man the occupant of the Oval Office was. After all, it is incontrovertible that Nixon wholeheartedly supported Israel throughout his presidency, that he never made any sort of antisemitic comment in public, and that he never took any measure likely to discriminate against American Jews.

The fact remains that Kissinger's propension to tolerating the most abject comments by the president crystallised criticism of him. Many American Jews saw in him the modern figure of the 'archetypal court Jew', prepared to draw a discreet veil over his Jewishness to pander to the prince.[8] In fact, Kissinger frequently asked his Jewish colleagues to stay away from meetings with the president so as not to irritate him.[9] But more than his attitude to Nixon, it was some of the stances Kissinger took in office which caused consternation.

In late summer 1973, tensions between the White House and Congress were at their peak. To pull off his policy of Détente, Kissinger wanted to grant the USSR most favoured nation status as quickly as possible. But numerous members of Congress were opposed to this and wanted to make the pursuit of Détente conditional on freedom of emigration for Soviet Jews by way of the Jackson–Vanik amendment to the 1974 Trade Act. Many Soviet Jews suffered persecution, but officially the Kremlin was opposed to them leaving to go to Israel and, to a lesser extent, the United States. For Kissinger, the situation of the Soviet Jews was a domestic issue that should in no way interfere with the policy of rapprochement with Moscow. This policy was his answer to an issue that he felt was of much greater concern to the United States: the risk of mutually destructive nuclear conflict between the two superpowers.

It was in this context that, on 1 September 1973, Kissinger said to Nixon: 'The emigration of Jews from the Soviet Union is not an objective of American foreign policy. And if they put Jews into gas chambers in the Soviet Union, it is not an American concern. Maybe a humanitarian concern.'[10] Then, to discredit the lobbying of Congress by certain American Jewish organisations, he played upon the president's antisemitic inclinations: 'I think that the Jewish community in this country on that issue is behaving unconscionably. It's behaving traitorously.'[11]

The master of American diplomacy justified such shocking language by his realist approach to foreign policy. For Kissinger, freedom of emigration for Soviet Jews was not a subject for which it was worth imperilling the policy of Détente. Above all, he felt that a more discreet diplomatic approach, which danced around the sensitivities of the men in the Kremlin, and which had already enabled the number of Soviet Jews emigrating to Israel to increase from 232 in 1968 to nearly 40,000 in 1972, was more effective than a public condemnation of the USSR by Congress.[12]

Kissinger also drew the ire of many American Jews in his battle with the United States ambassador to the United Nations, Daniel Patrick Moynihan, who had striven fiercely to prevent the UN General Assembly adopting a resolution, supported by Moscow, which determined Zionism to be a form of racism. The stirring speech given by Moynihan on 10 November 1975 in defence of Zionism earned him the admiration of the American Jewish community. Secretary of State Kissinger, however, viewed Moynihan's speech as a premeditated attack to undermine his policy of Détente. What's more, he was not too enamoured of seeing one of his ambassadors taking the limelight. The day of Moynihan's speech, Kissinger scornfully declared: 'We are conducting foreign policy. (...) This is not a synagogue.'[13] Then, with some irony, he wondered whether Moynihan – a Catholic of Irish origin – was deploying such considerable energy because he wished to convert to Judaism. Eight months after being named UN ambassador, Moynihan was relieved of his post.

Perhaps the best proof of Kissinger's tortured relationship with his Jewish heritage was his highly ambiguous relationship with Israel. He was capable of forging close links with antisemitic heads of state but, paradoxically, had much more difficulty in establishing a relationship of trust with the main Israeli leaders, whether Golda Meir, Moshe Dayan, Yitzhak Rabin or Shimon Peres. Numerous Israelis and American Jews reproached him for his Machiavellian manoeuvrings during the Yom Kippur War of 1973, which, in their view, delayed Israel's victory, thereby pointlessly killing and wounding many more young Israeli soldiers. The truth is that Kissinger never imagined that the IDF (Israel Defense Forces) might be vanquished. As he would emphasise on many occasions after leaving office: 'The security of Israel is a moral imperative for all free peoples.'[14] But nor did he wish for Israeli troops to inflict too resounding a defeat on the Arab armies, particularly that of Egypt's Anwar Sadat. Such a clear Israeli victory would have rendered the Jewish State less malleable and less dependent on the United States. That, Kissinger could never accept.

Just as many Europeans frequently complained that Kissinger no longer defended the interests of the continent of his birth despite his German origins, many Israelis and American Jews had trouble understanding how the first ever Jewish secretary of state could not at least appear to be a zealous defender of Israel's interests.

The reasons behind Henry Kissinger's attitude are twofold. He explained the first to the leaders of the principal American Jewish organisations just a few days before he left office. After recognising the 'very complicated relationship' he had with his fellow Jews, he went on to say: 'From my point of view, probably no criticism has hurt me more than if it came from this community. And probably from your point of view, it was especially painful if disagreements occurred between the Jewish community and the first Jewish secretary of state in American history.' Nevertheless, he said: 'I thought it was important for the future of Israel and for the future of the Jewish people, that the actions that the United States Government took were not seen to be the result of a special, personal relationship, but that the support we gave Israel reflected not my personal preferences alone, but the basic national interests of the United States.'[15]

As for the second reason, it is summed up in what Kissinger told Golda Meir one day: 'Golda, you must remember that first I am an American, second I am secretary of state and third I am a Jew.'[16]

Lee Kuan Yew

One drizzly winter evening in Paris, I went to meet a man who had been a close friend of Kissinger for many years. As I asked him about the figures who had influenced the master of American diplomacy, I expected him to mention Rockefeller, Nixon, Zhou Enlai or Sadat. Nothing of the sort. 'If you really want to understand Henry,' he suggested, 'you must look at Lee Kuan Yew.' Then he added: 'Not only are they both giants who will be remembered long after they're dead, they shared an intellectual and personal bond that says much about Henry.'

So began my quest to understand what drew these two seemingly very different men together. What could a German Jewish refugee have in common with the founding father of Singapore? What was the nature of the relationship between Kissinger and the man who turned a poverty-stricken third-world port into one of the world's premier economic powers? Why were the lives of these two men, whom Graham Allison considered 'two certifiable grand masters of international strategy in the last half century',[1] so closely intertwined?

Born just a few months apart in 1923, Lee and Kissinger were both very young when they experienced the collapse of the balance of powers and the reign of barbarism. A teenage Kissinger witnessed, powerless, the increasing stranglehold of the Nazi regime and the rise of antisemitism and hatred in the country of his birth, which he would flee in fear. As for Lee, he was about to commence his university studies when Japan invaded Singapore. Suddenly, the myths of the invincibility of the British Army and the superiority of the white man proved to be just that: myths. Four nightmarish years would follow for Lee and his family. The Imperial Japanese Army proceeded with the systematic extermination of all those they considered hostile among Singapore's Chinese population. This succession of purges and mass killings was called the Sook Ching. Tens of thousands of Singaporeans were slaughtered in this way. Lee himself was violently beaten one day for failing to prostrate himself before some passing Japanese soldiers.

Thousands of miles apart, Lee and Kissinger had each experienced evil up close. They had seen cultured, refined people become murderers, and had understood that human barbarity is without limit. As reticent as they were to talk about what they'd been through, they would draw from it a profound pessimism about human nature and the lessons of history.

Both men also witnessed the culpable blindness and the cowardice of democracies in the face of emerging tyrannies. They saw how powerless the 'civilised' nations were to prevent the most monstrous crimes. Never again would Lee and Kissinger place their faith in eloquent declarations of principle by statesmen, such as when Neville Chamberlain returned from Munich promising 'peace for our time'. Nor did they believe that the supposed wisdom of the masses would necessarily prevent the worst happening again. The Singaporean and the American had suffered too much from the madness of those very same masses and a collective pusillanimity not to be convinced that the guiding light often comes from lone figures such as de Gaulle and Churchill.

In the face of authoritarian regimes and the omnipotent tendencies of certain tyrants, Lee and Kissinger shared a conviction that democracies were fooling themselves if they thought they could preserve the world order through the primacy of the rule of law, which had proved to be a shield neither for the Jews of Europe nor for the populations of Asia who suffered torture, rape and murder at the hands of Japanese soldiers.

Above all, Lee and Kissinger realised that peace and

prosperity are as precious as they are fragile, for they are never guaranteed. In fact, they remain the exception and must be fought for constantly. More than a simple intellectual stance, this belief was deeply embedded in the psyches and bodies of the two men.

Lee and Kissinger met for the first time in 1967, when Singapore had been a free, independent state for two years. Lee, then prime minister, was invited to dinner with several members of the Harvard faculty. Discussion soon turned to the war in Vietnam. One after another, the eminent professors lambasted the current US policy, described President Johnson as a 'criminal' and a 'psychopath', and were unanimous in calling for a withdrawal of American troops. Kissinger, however, said nothing.

After politely listening to them each in turn, Lee spoke. 'You make me sick!' he declared. His fellow diners sat there stunned.[2]

Although Lee did not support the war in and of itself, he was convinced that his country's survival depended on the United States' unshakeable determination to create the conditions for a balance of powers in Asia. Given the hegemonic aims of the Communist tyrannies, the war in Vietnam was therefore a necessary evil to show the Kremlin and Beijing that they could not place the entire Asian continent under their yoke with impunity. This was an essential condition for Lee's city-state to be able to continue to freely pursue its own future. In the scornful, ironic criticisms levelled by his dinner companions, the Singaporean leader detected a thoughtlessness that could have tragic repercussions for his country.

Lee distrusted the bien-pensant American liberal elites who called for a policy of American isolationism. Like Kissinger, he had not forgotten that, throughout the 1930s, many of them had opposed their country joining any war against Nazi Germany or Imperial Japan.

Kissinger was struck that evening by Lee's courage and vision and admired his 'singular strategic acumen'.[3] The two men also shared a recognition of the importance of looking to the past. 'If you do not know history,' wrote Lee, 'you think short term. If you know history, you think medium and long term.'[4]

That Harvard dinner marked the start of a friendship that Kissinger would describe as 'one of the great blessings of my life'.[5] Over the five decades that followed, the two men would see each other dozens of times, particularly on Lee's frequent trips to the United States. During each visit, numerous high officials, both Democrat and Republican, would request an audience with Lee, all seeking precious advice from the man who, to quote Kissinger, had become 'a kind of conscience to leaders around the globe'.[6]

Year after year, Lee reminded them that they could not escape the responsibilities incumbent upon them as the world's leading superpower. He was not blind to America's faults. As a keen observer of American democracy, he was well aware of its institutional weaknesses, its deeply inegalitarian nature and the racial divisions running through its society. But he shared with Kissinger the conviction that the world's peace and prosperity depended upon the willingness of the United States to fully play its role on the global geopolitical chessboard in order to ensure, as his friend put it, 'a balance of power that enforces restraint where rules break down'.[7]

But Lee was also the man who 'explained China' to the American leadership. He possessed an intimate knowledge of this country, nourished by the close ties he took pains to maintain with successive Chinese leaders. From Deng Xiaoping to Xi Jinping, all of them called Lee a 'mentor'.

Lee Kuan Yew had understood from very early on that China's ambition was to erode American influence in Asia in order to assume the mantle of uncontested master of the continent. But rather than seeking to divert Beijing from its objectives – which he knew was impossible – Lee instead chose to make the American leadership aware of a truth that many of them did their best to ignore: that they would one day have to confront a superpower that was their equal both economically and militarily. 'I have had the privilege of meeting many world leaders over the past half century,' Kissinger wrote one day. 'None, however, has taught me more than Lee Kuan Yew.'[8]

As one of the few world leaders to be admired equally in Washington and in Beijing, Lee aimed to be an intermediary between the world's two leading superpowers. Above all, he wished to avoid Sino–American relations falling into the Thucydides Trap, which supposes that whenever an emerging power challenges the dominance of a ruling power, war will tend to ensue.

It seems clear that no foreign leader had as much influence as Lee on American foreign policy in relation to China. From the rapprochement conducted by Nixon and Kissinger to Obama's 'pivot to Asia', every major diplomatic initiative by Washington regarding Beijing has borne his fingerprint.

As the years passed, Lee and Kissinger came to share a common vision on many significant geostrategic challenges. Yet these two men remained the products and embodiments of two political systems whose rivalry has only accentuated over time.

For Kissinger, who had known the horror of the Nazi regime, democracy was what allowed him to know freedom anew, to walk fearlessly in the street and to build a new life in a country that was not his own. He was all too aware of what was precious about it. His love for America was simply inseparable from his attachment to democracy.

Lee, however, who had himself laid the foundations for an authoritarian regime in Singapore, was often a merciless critic of what Churchill once described as 'the worst form of Government except for all those other forms that have been tried from time to time'.[9]

When you have popular democracy, to win votes you have to give more and more. And to beat your opponent in the next election, you have to promise to give more away. So it is a never-ending process of auctions – and the cost, the debt being paid for by the next generation. Presidents do not get re-elected if they give a hard dose of medicine to their people. So, there is a tendency to procrastinate, to postpone unpopular policies in order to win elections. So, problems such as budget deficits, debt, and high unemployment have been carried forward from one administration to the next.[10]

In this light, it is striking to observe that Lee and Kissinger were players in a world where the prevailing assumption for a long time was that democracy would become the norm. After the fall of the Berlin Wall, the 'end of history' (as Francis Fukuyama announced) seemed inevitable.[11] It was predicted that the authoritarian regimes would fall one after another and that democracy would triumph everywhere.

But the return of power politics put an end to the illusion of linear history. In a new era of empires and geopolitical competition, the hope for the rapid triumph of democracies has dissipated. Throughout the world, many leaders are now inspired by the writings and achievements of Lee Kuan Yew. Paul Kagame and Nursultan Nazarbayev did not look to Western democracies to build the future of Rwanda and Kazakhstan, but rather to Lee's Singapore. They hoped to unlock a brighter future for their country by drawing clear – and sometimes explicit – inspiration from his implementation of an authoritarian regime that went hand in hand with a development model based on education, the fight against corruption, and meritocracy.

The reason why the Singaporean model has become so seductive is that Lee succeeded in transforming a little port of fewer than 2 million inhabitants into an international financial centre with triple that population in the space of a generation. In just fifty years, the per capita income has risen from $925 in

1970 to $85,000 in 2023.¹² Today, Singapore is seen as a model of urban and technological innovation, a country leading the way in several sectors, including health and education.

Although Lee and Kissinger had different relationships with democracy, they were in agreement on one point. It is as illusory as it is dangerous to try to impose an institutional system on a country that, by its history, is not familiar with it. In this respect, the vision of the American neoconservatives, whose ambition is to impose democracy by force on peoples who have never known it, was anathema to both the Singaporean leader and Kissinger.

In the eulogy he wrote in homage to Lee, Kissinger went as far as to suggest that the choice of a political regime other than that established by his friend might have driven Singapore to a dire fate. 'Lee's domestic methods fell short of the prescriptions of current US constitutional theory,' he euphemistically conceded. 'This is not the occasion to debate what other options were available. Had Singapore chosen the road of its critics, it might well have collapsed among its ethnic groups, as the example of Syria teaches today.'¹³

As deeply attached as Kissinger was to the democracy of his adopted land, these lines reveal, for neither the first time nor the last, his conviction that it was not the vocation of the United States to export or impose this system of government abroad.

In early 2015, when he learned that the Singaporean leader's health had suddenly deteriorated, Kissinger offered to visit him. Lee, out of a certain sense of propriety, refused. On 23 March 2015, Lee died. His friend immediately flew to Singapore. At the funeral, Henry could not hold back his tears.

Henry had lost more than a friend. Between the German Jewish refugee and the ethnic Chinese Singaporean, a brotherly bond had formed, for these two men were united in the deep conviction that the evils of history could resurface at any time.

Indeed, not long before he died, Lee expressed his fears that man had forgotten the lessons of the past. 'I was also troubled by the apparent over-confidence of a generation that has only known stability, growth and prosperity. I thought our people should understand how vulnerable Singapore was and is, the dangers that beset us, and how we nearly did not make it. Most of all, I hope that they will know that honest and effective government, public order and personal security, economic and social progress did not come about as the natural course of events.'[14]

With Lee Kuan Yew's death, the world lost a man who had helped to make it a safer place. Nobody was more aware of this than his American 'brother'.

Mentor

The heat was stifling. It was a summer day in 1944 at Camp Claiborne, in the heart of Louisiana, and the 84th Infantry Division was on final manoeuvres before embarking to go and fight in Europe. Twenty-one-year-old Private Kissinger was worn out, having just completed a gruelling training march with his company under the blazing sun. Stretched out on the ground, trying to get his breath back, he was suddenly raised from his torpor by a strident voice with a strong German accent: 'Who is in command here?'

The voice belonged to a diminutive private who had just alighted from a Jeep. A somewhat unnerved lieutenant colonel stepped forward: 'I am in charge here, private.' The private didn't miss a beat: 'Sir, I am sent by the general and I am going to speak to your company about why we are in this war.' He then proceeded to launch into an impassioned lecture on the Nazi menace and the need for young Americans to cross the Atlantic to fight in the name of freedom.[1]

The private's name was Fritz Kraemer, and Henry Kissinger was spellbound. He, more than any of the young soldiers surrounding him, was all too familiar with the atrocities that had turned Europe into a pit of barbarism. But for the first time in his military service, here was someone who knew how to find the right words to describe the feelings that drove him.

The next morning, he decided to send a message to this orator who had impressed him so much. 'I heard you speak yesterday. This is how it should be done. Can I help you somehow?'[2]

Kissinger didn't know it yet, but this message would change his life.

Henry Kissinger

*

Kraemer was born in 1908 in Essen, in the heart of the Ruhr. Son of a prosecutor and heir to a large family of industrialists, he was raised with a strong and devoted faith in both the Lutheran Church and the House of Hohenzollern. His flamboyant character came to the fore from an early age. Deeply patriotic, he had as much disdain for the communists as he did the Nazis, in whom he saw the negation of the Germanic identity. As a young man, he readily indulged in punch-ups with the gangs of Hitler Youths who sowed terror through Germany's streets.

None of this stopped Kraemer from completing university studies at the highest level, first in Berlin, then in Geneva and at the London School of Economics, before obtaining doctorates in law and political science at the universities of Frankfurt and Rome. When Hitler became chancellor in 1933, Kraemer moved to Italy, where he worked as senior legal advisor to the League of Nations, and was well placed to see the horror of Mussolini's regime and the spread of fascism across the continent. Above all, he gradually understood that if he wished to continue to uphold his own personal values, he now had no choice but to go into exile. This he did in 1939, leaving behind his wife and their young son, and travelling to the United States. As Kissinger would later comment: 'We were both refugees from Germany, I by necessity, Kraemer by choice.'[3]

In April 1943, armed with his cane, his ever-present monocle and his two doctorates, Kraemer joined the US Army as a simple private. But it didn't take long for General Bolling, who commanded Camp Claiborne, to notice this man with his distinguished bearing who barked orders at his comrades in German to get them used to future theatres of operations. Not long after being assigned to the camp's general headquarters, Kraemer made a surprising request to Bolling: 'We've got 2,800 new intellectuals in this division. Permit me to address them; otherwise, they will not understand why they are here.'[4]

Mentor

*

This is how Kraemer and Kissinger found themselves having a face-to-face sit-down several weeks later. Intrigued by the latter's suitably flattering message, Kraemer had invited Kissinger to dinner, where he was swiftly won over by his fellow countryman's exceptional intelligence. But it was something else that really struck Kraemer.

> Henry has great intelligence. But there are many people with great intelligence. This is not what sets Henry apart at all. He has something else, something beyond intelligence, and that makes him a genius. The best way I can describe it is that Henry Kissinger is musically attuned to history. This is not something you can learn, no matter how intelligent you are. It is a gift from God.[5]

Kraemer could also not help but feel a deep affection for this young man who, like him, had had to flee that Germany he loved and missed so much.

Over the following months, the two men spent an increasing amount of time together. Each night, amid the ruins of the European towns where they were stationed, they spent long hours discussing politics and the meaning of history. The young Kissinger soaked up the knowledge and clearly affirmed convictions of his new teacher like a sponge.

Talking about this period many years later, Kissinger would recount how 'Kraemer spoke of history and post-war challenges in his stentorian voice' and that he 'awakened my interest in political philosophy, inspiring my undergraduate and graduate theses'; before adding: 'Fritz Kraemer was the greatest single influence of my formative years.'[6]

Kissinger was enthralled by Kraemer's personality during those war years. He was particularly impressed by Kraemer's passionate adherence to his principles. In his eyes, Kraemer embodied absolute resistance to the Nazi regime. What contrast with his father, Louis Kissinger, whose almost naive kindness was a weakness, even a fault, in those tragic times.

Taken prisoner by the Germans during the Battle of the Bulge, Kraemer once again demonstrated a panache that inspired the admiration of his young disciple. Employing all his powers of persuasion, he convinced his German gaolers that an Allied victory was imminent and that it was in their best interests to give themselves up. And so this prisoner of war found himself the liberator of the town of Geilenkirchen, the control of which was handed to him by the offices of the Wehrmacht. Kraemer's distinctive mix of bravery and flamboyance was apparent again several months later when the 84th Infantry Division met the Red Army on the Elbe. As the US and Soviet troops tensely faced off in a prefiguration of their future Cold War rivalries, Kraemer gleefully defied them in a frenetic display of Cossack dancing.

As for Kissinger, Kraemer grew most attached to this young Jewish refugee who was unlike any other soldier. Having decided to make him his protégé, Kraemer appointed Kissinger to Bolling's general staff, then let him join the counter-espionage department. Above all, Kraemer made his young disciple aware of his huge potential.

To a journalist who described him one day as 'the man who discovered Kissinger', Kraemer emphatically replied: 'My role was not discovering Kissinger! My role was getting Kissinger to discover himself!'[7]

Kraemer's influence on Kissinger would last long after their years of army service. As Kissinger's deployment in Germany drew to its close, Kraemer gave him one last piece of advice: 'You need an education. Go to a fine college. A gentleman does not go to the City College of New York (referring to the institution where Kissinger had studied accounting at evening classes for two years before joining the army), he goes to Harvard.'[8] Such a recommendation could not fail to resonate strongly with a young man who now nurtured some very great ambitions. A few months later, Kissinger enrolled at Harvard.

Over the following years, the two men retained a special bond. Of course, Kissinger sought out new mentors. All had spellbinding characters, outsized egos and devastating charisma. These mentors included William Yandell Elliott at Harvard, and Nelson Rockefeller, who guided Kissinger through his first steps into politics and New York high society. The fact remains that Henry continued to consult Kraemer on every important decision he had to make.

Yet this link would be progressively stretched very thin indeed beneath the weight of strategic disagreements. The quagmire of Vietnam had convinced Kissinger that American public opinion was weary of wars and American interventionism. With the consent of Nixon then Ford, Kissinger therefore decided to pursue a policy of Détente with the USSR, the aim of which was eventually to create a balance of powers, which he felt would guarantee stability. It was this policy that would cause the split between the man people nicknamed 'the Prussian' and his former pupil.

For Kraemer, who had become an influential figure at the Pentagon, this policy was more than a strategic error. He saw in it a moral fault similar to the policy of appeasement pursued in the 1930s by certain European governments in the face of the rise of fascism. In 1975, Gerald Ford decided to sack Kissinger's great rival and a fervent opponent of Détente, the secretary of defense, James Schlesinger. This was the last straw for Kraemer, who decided to sever all contact with the man who was now secretary of state.

'As a human being you have to stand for political values,' Kraemer explained to justify his attitude. 'People must know that I do not approve of him [Kissinger]. This is a political-ethical stance.'[9]

Attempts at mediation by Nancy Kissinger came to naught.

Henry Kissinger

Kissinger and Kraemer did not speak to each other for twenty-eight years.

The split was deeply painful for both men. Henry lost his first mentor, a person he had been able to count on since the age of twenty-one. And Kraemer lost the man who had become like a son to him.

Questioned about this split decades later, Kissinger would say: 'Like the ancient prophets, he [Kraemer] made no concessions to human frailty or to historic evolution; he treated intermediate solutions as derogation from principle. And therein lay the source of our later estrangement. (...) For the prophet, there can be no gap between conception and implementation; the policymaker must build the necessary from the possible. (...) The prophet thinks in terms of crusades; the policymaker hedges against the possibility of human fallibility.'[10]

Yet the personal relationship that bound both men was too powerful for their paths not to cross again. In 2002, Kissinger took the decision to pick up the phone and call the man who, more than anyone, would forever be his mentor.[11]

Barely a year later, Kraemer died, aged ninety-five. On 8 October 2003, at Arlington Cemetery, his adopted country buried him with the highest military honours, and Kissinger paid a final homage to his teacher. Despite their past rifts, he acknowledged that Kraemer would always remain a 'beacon' for him.[12]

Metternich

'Metternich is not my hero!' Kissinger would insist.[1] Perhaps he was being honest. It's always a delicate thing to model yourself on someone to whom you bear a strong resemblance – someone who forever reminds you not only of your qualities but also of your own limits.

With that in mind, he would probably have preferred to be compared to Bismarck. Yet it was not the Iron Chancellor he felt closest to, but rather that master of intrigue, Metternich.

Henry Kissinger was still quite young when he began to take an interest in the man who was the great architect of post-Napoleonic Europe. He found the analysis of institutions to be too conceptual and abstract for his liking. Instead, convinced that he himself was destined for an exceptional existence, Kissinger took immense pleasure in discerning the imperfections, the intuitions, the strokes of genius and the fault lines that shaped the lives of great men. In studying their successes, their failures and – especially – their ability to recover from the toughest tests, he greedily sought the keys to his own future.

It was therefore quite natural that Kissinger made Metternich the central figure of his undergraduate dissertation (1957) alongside Viscount Castlereagh. In it, he sketches the following portrait of the Austrian prince:

> Equally at home in the salon and in the Cabinet, graceful and facile, he was the *beau-ideal* of the eighteenth-century aristocracy which justified itself not by its truth but by its existence. And if he never came to terms with the new age

Henry Kissinger

> it was not because he failed to understand its seriousness but because he disdained it. Therein too his fate was the fate of Austria. It was this man who for over a generation ruled Austria, and often Europe, with the same methods of almost nonchalant manipulation he had learned in his youth. (...) He would have moved through the drawing-rooms of the fashionable world with his undeniable charm and grace, subtly and aloofly conducting his diplomacy with the circuitousness which is a symbol of certainty, of a world in which everybody understands intangibles in the same manner. (...) His genius was instrumental, not creative; he excelled at manipulation, not construction. Trained in the school of the eighteenth-century cabinet diplomacy, he preferred the subtle manoeuvre to the frontal attack, while his rationalism frequently made him mistake a well-phrased manifesto for an accomplished action. (...) This, then, was the statesman to whom Austria's fate was entrusted in 1812: doctrinaire, but in the universalist manner of the eighteenth century; devious, because the very certainty of his convictions made him extremely flexible in his choice of means; matter-of-fact and aloof; coldly pursuing the art of statecraft. His characteristic quality was tact, the sensibility to nuance. Such a man might have dominated the eighteenth century, but he was formidable in any age.[2]

These lines are a stinging rebuttal to those who doubt that when people write about other people, they are often writing about themselves.

As a young Harvard professor, Kissinger's interest in Metternich continued, in both his research and his teaching. His class on 'Principles of international relations' featured the Austrian prince heavily, as Kissinger would discourse at length, and with scintillating erudition, on the Austrian diplomat's career. His students listened, rapt. More than 200 of them would cram into

Metternich

a small lecture hall to drink up the words and deadly wit of this charismatic professor.

But it was also in the highest spheres of power that Metternich continued to be a loyal and valued companion for Kissinger. When he boarded a plane to Saigon in August 1972 for crucial negotiations with Thiệu on Vietnam's future, Kissinger took a biography of Metternich with him, barely lifting his nose from the page throughout the long flight. In the most intense periods, when he was under ever increasing pressure, he knew that Metternich could always furnish answers to the challenges of the moment.

More than anyone else, it was Metternich who taught Kissinger that the keys to a diplomat's success are to be found in their own personality.

Napoleon considered that, when it came to Metternich, the line between politics and subterfuge was more than blurred. It would be hard to think otherwise of Henry Kissinger, who became an undisputed master of ruse and cunning. Indeed when he commented that 'sometimes the art of diplomacy is to keep the obvious obscured',[3] Kissinger was paying fierce homage to the Austrian statesman.[4]

Yitzhak Rabin, tragically assassinated in 1995, said that 'Kissinger had a Metternichian system of telling only half the truth.' Not without humour, the Israeli prime minister added that the flamboyant American diplomat 'didn't lie. He would have lost credibility. He didn't tell the whole truth.'[5]

The Israelis had many opportunities, mainly around the Yom Kippur War, to observe the talents of the secretary of state up close. Shimon Peres explained: 'If you didn't listen word by word, you could be carried away by what he said. But if you listened word by word, he wasn't lying.' This did not, however, make Peres trust Kissinger. He once confided privately about him to Rabin in terms that leave no room for ambiguity. 'With due respect to Kissinger, he is the most devious man I've ever met.'[6]

*

Kissinger learned the art of cunning from Metternich. But both men also shared a common view of history.

The tragic experiences of his youth had tinged Kissinger's worldview with a deep intellectual pessimism. He acquired the belief that all civilisations are inexorably destined to fall into decadence and vanish. He drew the same conclusion as Metternich that, in light of this, a diplomat's role was first and foremost to avoid the power one serves tipping into a decline. One maintains one's influence, therefore, through 'diplomatic pirouettes'.

Nazism had allowed Kissinger to view all too closely the consequences of chaos. As a result, he developed a visceral aversion to all revolutionary movements. Like Metternich, this made him a conservative to his bones. But mindful of never confusing morals with politics, Kissinger made sure never to fall into ideology. He remained a pragmatist, as Metternich was in his time. Indeed, he wrote of the Austrian diplomat that he 'represented eternal principles not a system'.[7]

But it was also under circumstances that were, on the face of it, more surprising, that Metternich was of great help to his disciple. Kissinger must surely have thought often about the relationship between the Austrian chancellor and Emperor Francis I in the course of the subtle manoeuvring that was part and parcel of the incredibly complex, even perverse, relationship he had with Nixon – and on which his entire career hinged. In studying Metternich's turbulent relationship with the man he served, Kissinger could not fail to have memorised solutions to overcome the difficulties and pitfalls facing him in the corridors of the White House.

Nor can it have escaped Kissinger that when Metternich became foreign minister in 1809, Austria had recently been humiliated repeatedly by the Napoleonic armies. As Kissinger wrote in his dissertation, it was an empire 'which had lost its élan and its self-confidence, which knew its limits but hardly its goals'.[8] The parallel with the America of 1969, bogged down in the Vietnam War, was striking.

Like Nixon and Kissinger a century and a half later, Francis I and Metternich were convinced that they lacked sufficient domestic support to pursue a foreign policy that was frank and transparent. These two duos had no choice if they were to shape the global balance: they had to develop a foreign policy in which the arts of dupery, intrigue and cunning would play a decisive role. As Kissinger analysed it: 'Since Austrian policy could not draw its strength from the inspiration of its people, it had to achieve its aims by the tenacity and subtlety of its diplomacy.'[9]

Yet despite the similarities shared by Metternich and Kissinger, there are some major differences between these two giants of diplomacy. Whereas Metternich reigned supreme over the diplomacy of the Austrian Empire for nearly four decades, Kissinger was in office for only eight years.

On 12 December 1976, as his plane climbed out of London to take him back to Washington for the last time as secretary of state, it is probable that Kissinger felt a touch of envy for the Austrian prince. Kissinger knew, more than anyone, that great men require time to leave their mark on history. Is it not time that truly separates Kissinger for all eternity from the man who, if not his hero, was his biggest inspiration?

Nixon

10 November 1967. The evening is just getting going in this superb Fifth Avenue apartment when Henry Kissinger makes his appearance. The hostess, Clare Boothe Luce, has invited an impressive array of captains of industry, figures of high finance and members of the New York intelligentsia. Clare is a playwright, journalist, and a former congresswoman and diplomat, as well as the widow of the press magnate Henry Luce. Invitations to her soirées are among the most highly sought in all New York, and tonight she is laser-focused on making the introduction between two men she admires greatly: Henry Kissinger and Richard Nixon.

But Henry is bored. He knows no one and the evening is dragging on. Just as he's getting ready to leave, Richard Nixon finally turns up. Clare leads the pair into the library, off to the side. And it is in this room, the walls of which are hung with paintings by Frida Kahlo, that Nixon and Kissinger talk for the first time.

Nixon had experienced a long spell in the wilderness following not only his defeat to Kennedy in the presidential election of 1960 but also (and above all) his humiliating failure to win the governorship of California in 1962. However, he had put the intervening years to good use: reading, travelling and refining his vision of the major global issues. Little by little, the image of the rugged, unscrupulous politician shifted into that of a statesman who had learned from his failures. As Thanksgiving 1967 approached, Nixon increasingly appeared as a possible solution to an America deeply divided by the war in Vietnam and shaken by the race riots that had exploded across the country that summer.

As for Kissinger, he now enjoyed a level of renown that extended far beyond the fusty circles of academia. Indeed, back in 1957, vice president Nixon himself had been photographed holding a copy of Kissinger's first book, *Nuclear Weapons and Foreign Policy*. And in 1959, he penned an appreciative letter to Kissinger congratulating him on an article in which he espoused a firm approach to the USSR.[1] Nixon was keen to meet the man who he knew to be a valued advisor to his rival, Nelson Rockefeller.

Lasting just a few minutes, their first encounter would leave a lasting impression on both men. Nixon was drawn to this young Harvard professor who did not adhere to the conformist bien-pensant idealism that reigned on Ivy League campuses, while Kissinger, full of negative preconceptions about Nixon, was impressed by the finesse of the man and the clarity of his analyses. As he would later admit to one of his friends, he found Nixon 'talked in a gentler way, a more thoughtful way' than he would have imagined.[2]

Still, Kissinger remained totally loyal to Rockefeller. Less than a year later, he cried tears of sadness and anger when his mentor was defeated in the Republican primaries. To those around him, he would say of Nixon: 'He is not fit to be President.'[3] And over the course of the presidential campaign, in which Nixon faced off against the Democratic candidate, Hubert Humphrey, Kissinger let it be known that he would be prepared to join an administration led by Humphrey. At a lunch in Paris with Daniel Davidson, a young diplomat serving in the Johnson administration, he even went so far as to say: 'Six days a week I'm for Hubert but on the seventh day, I think they're both awful.'[4]

On 22 November 1968, a few days after Richard Nixon's election to the White House, Nelson Rockefeller gathered his inner circle and asked them if he should agree to join the Nixon administration should he be offered the post of secretary of state or secretary of defense. Suddenly, the phone rang. It was Dwight Chapin, Nixon's personal aide. Everyone thought the call was for Nelson Rockefeller. In fact, it was Henry whom the future occupant of the White House wished to see as soon as possible.

Kissinger dashed out of Rockefeller's place on 54th Street and headed to the Hotel Pierre, just a few blocks away, where Nixon had set up his transition team on the 39th floor overlooking Central Park. The two men would spend three hours huddled in conclave.

Nixon began by laying out the diplomatic revolution he wished to pursue, not hiding his distrust, even aversion, to bureaucracy. As vice president under Eisenhower, he had felt disregarded by the pen pushers in the State Department and was intent on getting his own back. Above all, he shared with Kissinger the conviction that American officialdom was plagued by a form of 'intellectual constipation'. From Foggy Bottom to Langley and the Pentagon, new and audacious ideas were in very short supply. The State Department, the CIA and the Department of Defense seemed paralysed by a total aversion to risk.

Nixon wanted to shake things up by concentrating the power around himself. As he would later explain: 'From the outset of my administration, however, I planned to direct foreign policy from the White House.'[5] He and Henry both believed that it would be more efficient to bypass the bureaucracy rather than confront it.

To this end, Nixon wished to reinvigorate and reinforce the powers of the National Security Council. Attached directly to the White House, the body had been created by Harry Truman in 1947 to ensure coordination on foreign policy between the various government agencies. Its influence had, however, declined progressively under Kennedy and Johnson. For Nixon, the National Security Council must become a tool that would allow him to undertake daring acts of diplomacy built on secret initiatives and tactical actions that would be long-lasting in their effects.

An intellectual bond formed between the two men. Henry was won over by Nixon's vision, which chimed closely with his own. 'I was struck by his perceptiveness and knowledge so at variance with my previous image of him,' wrote Kissinger in his memoirs.[6] Yet during this first long meeting he also noticed Nixon's uneasiness, his shifty gaze. It was a striking contrast with his mentors, Kraemer, Elliott and Rockefeller, who all had immense charisma and unshakeable confidence in themselves. As the meeting drew to a close, Nixon, scared of rejection, didn't even dare make the slightest proposition to Kissinger, who left the Hotel Pierre somewhat baffled.

The next morning, though, Henry received two phone calls. The first was from Rockefeller informing him that Nixon had asked him to stay as governor of New York State – a not-so-subtle way of communicating that Nixon wouldn't be offering Rockefeller a post in his administration. The second, from the president-elect's personal aide, asked Kissinger to meet Nixon again at the Hotel Pierre.

And so it was, on 27 November, that Kissinger again found himself sitting opposite Nixon, who had finally resolved to offer him the much-coveted post of national security advisor. There then followed a surprising scene in which the man preparing to lead the world's leading superpower proceeded to 'sell' himself to his future advisor. In his bid to get Kissinger to accept the post, he even went so far as to urge him to get in touch with several professors at Duke University who would give Henry glowing reports of their former student.

Kissinger asked for a few days to think about it. He feared the reaction of his Harvard colleagues, whose disdain of Nixon he knew all too well and with whom he had never pulled any punches in his own criticism of the man. He was also aware that entering the White House would earn him the enduring hatred of Rockefeller's other advisors. But the post of national security advisor was the sort of opportunity you don't turn down. At best, Henry had been hoping to become director of policy planning at the State Department. Never would he have dreamed of becoming the president's closest diplomatic advisor so quickly.

In making his decision, Kissinger consulted two of his mentors. Fritz Kraemer warned him: 'The "right" will call you the Jew who lost Southeast Asia; the "left" will call you a traitor to the cause. But,' he added, 'as a citizen, of course, you have to take it.'[7] But it was Nelson Rockefeller's opinion that proved decisive. After giving Kissinger short shrift for having kept Nixon waiting for an answer, Rockefeller gave Henry $50,000 to compensate him for the income he would lose through choosing to join the administration. On 29 November 1968, Kissinger called Dwight Chapin to accept the president's offer.

This date marks the birth of one of the most powerful, yet also most surprising, duos in American political life. What did these two men actually have in common? Nixon would himself acknowledge that 'the combination was unlikely – the grocer's son from Whittier and the refugee from Hitler's Germany, the politician and the academic.'[8]

But it was not only their origins that appeared to set the Southern Californian Quaker boy and the New York Jewish refugee apart. At first glance, they appeared to have opposing, even incompatible, personalities. Though he knew how to whip up a crowd and grasp America's soul in order to get elected, Nixon detested any sort of social niceties. Shy and solitary, he withdrew into himself whenever difficulties appeared. If he felt attacked, he could become deeply listless and spend whole days in the Oval Office ruminating on vengeful comebacks.

Kissinger, however, had overcome the shyness of his youth and morphed into a seductive character eager for social interaction. He felt quite at ease (and would turn on all his charm) in the salons of those beautiful Georgetown residences that the president shunned like the plague. And whereas Kissinger was blessed with an analytical mind that enabled him to pore over the tiniest details of the issues he was dealing with, Nixon relied on a much more intuitive form of intelligence. All this led Pat Nixon, the president's wife, to conclude that it was a 'marriage of convenience' between her husband and Henry.

Yet it would be a mistake not to see that the two men were bound by something more than merely their shared interests. Kissinger may have been more extroverted than Nixon, but they both had deep feelings of insecurity and an unquenchable thirst for recognition. In what seemed to them to be a hostile world, the president and his advisor cultivated a taste for secrecy, compulsive suspicion and the consummate art of manipulation, both in diplomacy and in their personal relations. As Lawrence Eagleburger, one of the national security advisor's closest aides, pointed out: 'Kissinger and Nixon both had degrees of paranoia. It led them to worry about each other, but it also led them to make common cause on perceived mutual enemies.'[9]

Nixon and Kissinger, who saw each other as outsiders, were also driven by a huge ambition: to be the architects of a new international system in which they would assert the domination of the United States while reducing the hazards of the Cold War. The two men were prepared to sideline anyone who would prevent them fulfilling their destiny and going down in history as one of the most eminent couples in American foreign policy. Not bureaucracy, nor Congress, nor the traditional channels of diplomacy would stand in the way of the *Realpolitik* they wished to implement.

On 25 September 1969, when Golda Meir was making a state visit to Washington, Nixon explained their approach: 'Our Golden Rule as far as international diplomacy is concerned is: "Do unto others as they do unto you."' 'Plus 10 per cent,' added Kissinger quickly.[10]

But the main thing that united both men was their

immoderate taste for foreign policy. Nixon would often ask Kissinger to stay in the Oval Office after the morning briefing, whereupon they would spend several hours engaged in passionate discussion of geopolitical events, exploring possible strategic directions. Nixon, like Kissinger, was a man who lived and breathed diplomacy.

It was a complex, love–hate relationship in which the noblest aspirations were accompanied by the vilest behaviour. It resulted in courageous decisions that would leave their mark on history, but also the most scurrilous acts. Grandeur rubbed shoulders with mediocrity in Nixon and Kissinger's day-to-day. For five and a half years, the two most powerful men in the United States urged each other on, gripped by what the historian Robert Dallek described so appositely as 'autointoxication'.[11]

At the start of his presidency, Nixon's intellectual admiration for Kissinger was combined with a sense of satisfaction that he had snatched this advisor as a 'spoil of war' from Rockefeller. Having always felt disdained by the intellectual élites, he was proud of having enticed a Harvard academic into his orbit. At official dinners and visits by prestigious guests, Nixon would show him off almost like some performing monkey. The two men spoke several times a day and it took just a few months for Kissinger to become Nixon's most influential advisor.

But the ambitions and growing aura of this advisor soon began to niggle at Nixon. 'I don't trust Henry,' he told a friend, before adding, more to reassure himself than because he believed it, 'but I can use him.'[12] Kissinger's megalomania and his difficult nature also bothered him. Nixon would often discuss 'the Kissinger problem'[13] with the White House chief of staff, Bob Haldeman. Henry's recurrent fits of ego and his persistent quarrelling with Secretary of State William Rogers caused much torment to a president who hated having to manage personal conflicts.

Lastly, Nixon had a hunch that Kissinger was not too kind

about him at the Washington society parties he attended. He also suspected Kissinger of being responsible for numerous indiscretions and leaks, which sent him out of his mind. On both points, the president's intuition proved correct.

In private, Kissinger liked to present himself as the man who protected Nixon from his ghastlier instincts, thus avoiding many an error or instance of misconduct. He put about rumours that were less than complimentary of the figure he would often refer to as 'that madman' or, if he wished to highlight the president's penchant for alcohol, 'our drunken friend'. As Daniel Moynihan, Nixon's assistant for domestic policy, wrote: 'It was his [Kissinger's] obsession that no one *ever* should appear to be closer to the President than he, while neither should anyone be seen to hold this President in greater contempt.'[14]

In front of Nixon, though, Henry frequently showed an almost toadying deference. His past experiences had taught him the art of charming the powerful, and he knew full well the extent to which flattery, as flagrant as it might be, was key to soothing a president prone to fits of rage. White House Counsel John Ehrlichman described Kissinger as 'obsequious'. Before a speech on Vietnam in April 1971, Henry sent the following letter to the occupant of the Oval Office: 'No matter what the result, free people everywhere will be forever in your debt. Your serenity during crises, your steadfastness under pressure, have been all that have prevented the triumph of mass hysteria. It has been an inspiration to serve. As always, H.'[15] Peter G. Peterson, the assistant to the president for international economic affairs, also recalls discussions during which Kissinger never stopped criticising Nixon in the harshest terms. Suddenly, the phone would ring. On the other end of the line: Nixon. The only phrase Peterson now heard coming out of Kissinger's mouth was: 'Oh, yes, Mr President,' repeated ad infinitum in a fawning tone.[16]

Even when Nixon made antisemitic comments in front

of him and called him his 'Jew boy', Henry didn't react. He was convinced that opposing Nixon verbally would serve no purpose. Moreover, he would lose any opportunity to suppress Nixon's darker urges if he found himself cast out of the president's inner circle. He was all too aware of what happened to people who dared stand up to Nixon. The advisors Herb Klein and Robert Finch were unceremoniously sidelined, while William Rogers gradually lost the confidence of the president despite their friendship.

But despite Kissinger's extensive powers of seduction, Nixon's admiration for him became gradually tinged with envy and suspicions of disloyalty. An atmosphere of paranoia grew between the two men. Nixon began having his advisor bugged. As for Henry, he asked his secretaries and aides to listen secretly to his own phone calls with the president and then to make an exhaustive transcription of them. Nixon's bitterness and hostility increased alongside his dependence on Kissinger, which, as the president was well aware, grew stronger with every passing month.

If there is one trend that stands out clearly from the five and a half years the two men spent together, it is Kissinger's growing grip on US foreign policy. This was due to a combination of several factors, not least of which were Kissinger's intellectual abilities, his capacity for work and his knack for surrounding himself with the top talent, all of which soon made him indispensable. But Henry also made sure to keep at arm's length (or get rid of entirely) all those who might overshadow him, notably William Rogers and Morton Halperin.

Finally, the Watergate scandal considerably reinforced his influence. In an administration crumbling on all sides, Kissinger's huge popularity and intact reputation made him an essential player, unlike H.R. Haldeman and John Ehrlichman, who formed the president's inner circle and were forced to resign on 30 April 1973. Without his 'Prussians', Nixon found himself isolated at the White House. Above all, he was less and less capable of focusing on foreign policy issues.

Nixon's decline made Kissinger the unchallenged master of American diplomacy. Whenever the president shut himself away in his office or at Camp David, knocking back scotch after scotch and watching the film *Patton* on repeat, Henry found himself alone in charge. Such was the case with the bombing of Hanoi over Christmas 1972, when Nixon was unreachable. But it was during the outbreak of the Yom Kippur War that Kissinger's grip on foreign policy became clearest. On 6 October 1973, Egypt and Syria launched their surprise attack on Israel. The Israeli leadership informed Kissinger as early as six in the morning. But although some key decisions had to be taken immediately, he waited three and a half hours before briefing the president.

Yet Kissinger retained a deep affection for Nixon in spite of the rancour, the backstabbing and the jealousy that increasingly characterised their relationship. For Nixon was a man with many facets. As Henry would explain years later, different personalities coexisted and battled within the man he served. 'One was idealistic, thoughtful, generous; another was vindictive, petty, emotional.'[17]

On 7 August 1974, just after 6 p.m., Kissinger walked into the Oval Office. A crestfallen Nixon was looking out at the White House Rose Garden. Henry approached him and placed his hand on the president's shoulder. For two such emotionally reserved men, the gesture spoke volumes. A little later in the evening, the president told his advisor that he was resigning. Henry could not hold back his tears. A long moment passed, but as Kissinger was getting up to leave, Nixon asked him to stay and pray together with him.[18]

As much as he criticised Nixon – often harshly – Kissinger always acknowledged the great courage of which Nixon was sometimes capable when he had to take unpopular decisions. He saw something 'heroic' in Nixon despite the man's many

Nixon

faults, of which he was all too aware. At Nixon's funeral on 27 April 1994, Kissinger said the following: 'In the conduct of foreign policy, Richard Nixon was one of the seminal presidents. (...) He achieved greatly, and he suffered deeply. But he never gave up. In his solitude, he envisaged a new international order that would reduce lingering enmities, strengthen historic friendships and give new hope to mankind – a vision where dreams and possibilities conjoined.'[19]

Paula

Late February 1991 found Paula Kissinger in Puerto Rico where, for many years, she and her husband Louis had taken to fleeing the freezing New York winters for a few months. After the death of Louis in 1982, she continued, every year, to rent the little seaside apartment they loved so much.

That Saturday, Paula had dolled herself up. One of her grandsons had told her he was coming to visit, travelling all the way from California to spend a few days with her. He picked her up at the apartment at the agreed time and drove her to the Caribe Hilton where they were to have dinner. Imagine Paula's surprise when, upon arriving at the hotel, she found her two sons, Henry and Walter, waiting for her along with all the members of her family, come to celebrate her ninetieth birthday.

Henry Kissinger was never thought of as the sentimental type, except by his mother. Over the course of that evening, though, he told her something he had always kept to himself: 'In times of adversity, you were the one who held us together through your courage and spirit and devotion. Everything I have achieved, that our family has achieved, is due to you.' Paula looked from her son to those sitting around them and, after a moment of silence, replied: 'It was worth to have lived a life for.'[1]

Her eldest son was right. It was she who had taken the painful decision to leave their native country in August 1938 as the Nazi threat grew ever stronger. While Louis had remained blind to reality, Paula understood, as she saw her non-Jewish friends turn away as she passed by, that there was no future for her family in Germany.

'It was my decision', she explained many years later, 'and I did it because of the children. I knew there was not a life to be made for them if we stayed.'[2]

This decision was all the more heartrending because Paula's father (she was an only child) was dying of cancer. But in early summer 1938, she realised she could delay their departure no longer. The Kissingers paid a final visit to Falk Stern in his house in Leutershausen, a little village thirty miles from Nuremberg where Paula's grandfather had become a cattle dealer in the early nineteenth century. His son had taken over the business and made a success of it, becoming an important figure in the local Jewish community.

As he bade farewell to his father-in-law, Louis Kissinger could not hold back his tears. But despite her inner turmoil, Paula remained impassive. She wanted to stay strong for her two boys because she knew that the future of the family now depended upon her.

Paula and Louis had met in Fürth in the early 1920s. She was immediately charmed by this young schoolmaster who, though often lost in his thoughts, was so kind and so bright. Louis had been drawn to Paula's shrewdness, her sense of humour and her sparkling personality. Somewhat reserved, Louis loved this young woman's joie de vivre. In 1922, despite their age difference – Louis was thirty-five and Paula twenty-one – they got married.

Paula loved her husband deeply, but after Hitler's rise to power she sensed that she could not depend on Louis in such tricky times. 'He was a gentle man in a world with no place for gentleness,' Henry Kissinger once remarked about his father.[3]

Removed from his teaching post because of his Jewish heritage, Louis was convinced that this could only be a mistake and that he would soon get his job back. Like many German Jews who were deeply patriotic, he simply couldn't imagine his country persecuting him. He thought that the Nazi regime was nothing but a brief parenthesis.

It was therefore Paula who took the decision alone to emigrate with her family to a country she had never seen.

After arriving in New York, Louis Kissinger slumped into a long listlessness. He had lost his bearings amid a language and culture that were alien to him. The drop in social standing that resulted from the loss of his schoolmaster status was incredibly hard for him to bear. He felt adrift, useless, and spent his time pacing round their modest apartment in Washington Heights. The responsibility for feeding the family therefore fell on Paula.

She learned English very fast, then began working as a cook and a caterer. It was hard at first, but her tenacity and the zeal she put into her work started to bear fruit. It was thanks to her that her sons never went without and were able to go to university.

Those first years in New York marked the start of a long road that would reach a culmination thirty-five years later.

On 22 September 1973, Paula, looking radiant in an elegant white suit, stood in the East Room of the White House. She held in her hands the Bible on which her eldest son was preparing to swear the oath of office as the new secretary of state of the United States, watched by Richard Nixon, Kirk Douglas and Nelson Rockefeller.

Many guests struggled to hide their emotions that day. In Henry Kissinger, this refugee who had reached the apex of power, they saw the embodiment of the American dream. Unlike many of the others, Paula managed to hold back any tears of joy. Deep down, though, she was as proud as could be. Henry's success justified all the hardships, humiliations and efforts of the past few decades. But her mother's pride would never wipe from her memory the hatred that her kith and kin had suffered in their country of origin.

On 15 December 1975, Paula and Louis returned to Fürth at the invitation of the municipality, who had awarded Henry a

Henry Kissinger

Gold Medal for Distinguished Native Citizens.[4] Louis couldn't hide his joy. At a lunch with some old friends, he told them: 'We forget all the bad memories on this day.' Beside him, Paula remained silent and stony-faced. Unlike her husband, she could never forgive those who were now honouring her son. Asked by a reporter what she was feeling, she replied: 'In my heart, I knew they would have burned us with the others if we had stayed.'[5]

Despite her sons' repeated entreaties, Paula lived out the rest of her days in the same small apartment in Washington Heights, refusing to leave this home she had found for her family not long after arriving in New York. She died aged ninety-seven on 15 November 1998, surrounded by her two sons, six grandchildren and six great-grandchildren.

A few years before her death, Paula had a bad fall in her kitchen and lay there on her own and unconscious for several hours. When she was finally taken to hospital, the doctors immediately put her on life support. On arriving at her bedside, Henry was told that she would probably never wake up and, even if she did, that she wouldn't be able to speak and that her mental faculties would be seriously damaged. They suggested to Henry that the best thing would be to switch off the machines keeping her alive. Henry refused. 'You don't know my mother,' he told them. For several days, the medical prognosis seemed accurate: Paula remained in a coma. Then, one morning, she suddenly woke up, turned to her son, who was sitting close by, and asked: 'What day is it?' 'Tuesday,' a startled Henry answered. 'Cancel my 10 o'clock dentist appointment,' Paula said.[6]

Realpolitik

Kissinger's name is closely linked to the concept of *Realpolitik*. It is rare to find an article about the subject that fails to mention his name. It is also rare to come across a pen portrait of the diplomat that doesn't describe him, after barely a few lines, as a 'master' or 'apostle' of *Realpolitik*. In either case, however, it is even rarer for the term to be given a strict definition.

According to Kissinger's critics, the notion of *Realpolitik* suggests a mix of brutality and cynicism whose only goal is the realisation of an amoral policy. Indeed, his Harvard colleague and rival, Stanley Hoffmann, considered that Kissinger's career could be summed up as 'a quest for a *Realpolitik* devoid of moral homilies'.[1] In branding him a merciless practitioner of *Realpolitik*, Kissinger's detractors have already set out his bill of indictment, arguing that this *Realpolitik* masks some dreadful transgressions; even, according to his most draconian prosecutors, war crimes. The charge sheet details the secret bombing of Cambodia, the overthrow of Salvador Allende in Chile and the blind eye turned to atrocities in Bangladesh and in East Timor as evidence of the dark side of Kissingerian *Realpolitik*.

However, certain admirers of Kissinger imagine the concept of *Realpolitik* as a shrewd combination of pragmatism, lucidity and efficiency. It's the tool that enabled the man who led American diplomacy from 1969 to 1977 to achieve his greatest successes. The Sino–American Rapprochement, the policy of Détente, the Paris Peace Accords on Vietnam and the negotiations that ended the Yom Kippur War all illustrate the pertinence of Kissinger's *Realpolitik* in their eyes.[2]

Whether the term is employed as a label, a slogan or a course of action, *Realpolitik* is one of those portmanteau words used frequently yet little understood. It means whatever the individual wielding it wishes it to mean. A proper examination of the origin of the concept is therefore essential.

As the British historian John Bew reminds us, the term appeared for the first time in 1853, used by the German political activist August Ludwig von Rochau. Rochau defined *Realpolitik* as a method of action based upon a rational analysis of the factors determining a given situation. This analysis relies upon an understanding of the historical and political circumstances and of the power mindsets at work, as well as a precise evaluation of the strength of ideas and emotions involved. Devoid of any sort of self-delusion, inasmuch as that is possible, it facilitates decision-making to achieve not ideals but a concrete objective.[3]
— For Rochau, the objective was none other than the unification of Germany in a Europe jarred by the opposing forces of nationalism and liberalism. It is natural, therefore, that *Realpolitik* was initially embodied by the father of German unity, Otto von Bismarck. But in personifying it, the Iron Chancellor, whom Kissinger himself described as being 'unencumbered by moral scruples',[4] would also imbue this concept with certain characteristics commonly associated with him – namely Machiavellianism, immorality and cruelty – thus shifting *Realpolitik* away from its original definition.

It was only after the First World War that *Realpolitik* entered the arena of American political and intellectual debate. The liberal internationalism espoused by President Woodrow Wilson set its own idealism against the supposed 'cynicism' of *Realpolitik*. Later, in the years following the Second World War, the concept became central to American foreign policy, promoted by the writings of German-born academics such as Reinhold Niebuhr and Hans J. Morgenthau, and diplomats such as George Kennan. Consequently, in current everyday use, the term is synonymous with power politics stripped of all moral considerations and supported by a pessimistic view of human nature.

Can we therefore consider Kissinger to have been a practitioner of *Realpolitik*?

What is striking is how wary Kissinger appeared to be of this term. Like Bismarck, he made sure never to use the word when he was in power, conscious that the term would only be used to caricature his actions and evoke his European origins, thus implying that, in a sense, his politics ran contrary to American values and traditions.

In an interview given to *Der Spiegel* in 2009, Kissinger explained it as follows. 'Let me say a word about *Realpolitik*, just for clarification. I regularly get accused of conducting *Realpolitik*. I don't think I have ever used that term. It is a way by which critics want to label me and say: "Watch him. He's a German really. He doesn't have the American view of things."'[5] In 2012, he returned to the Manichaean connotations now associated with *Realpolitik*. 'The advocates of a realist foreign policy are caricatured with the German term *Realpolitik*, I suppose to facilitate the choosing of sides.'[6]

But beyond the distrust that Kissinger felt for the term, what can we glean from the sources of intellectual inspiration that helped fashion it?

Throughout his youth and his academic career, Kissinger pursued a particularly eclectic range of studies, which gave him the opportunity to develop his thinking through contact with figures who were in no way disciples of *Realpolitik*. His first mentor, Fritz Kraemer, took a moral view of foreign policy. At Harvard, Kissinger wrote his undergraduate dissertation on three thinkers – Emmanuel Kant, Oswald Spengler and Arnold Toynbee – who sit outside the realist tradition. As a student, he also attended the lectures of Carl J. Friedrich, a fierce critic of Hans Morgenthau and Reinhold Niebuhr, whom he saw as theoreticians of the 'American version of German *Realpolitik*'.[7] Later,

Henry Kissinger

Henry would also make his journal *Confluence* welcome to many authors championing a liberal vision of international affairs; among them, McGeorge Bundy, Paul Nitze and Hannah Arendt.

Gradually, however, Kissinger developed a realist view of foreign policy. As a pupil of Hans Morgenthau, who had a deep influence on him, Henry was fascinated by the work and character of the Iron Chancellor. In 1968, not long before setting foot in the corridors of power, he devoted a long article to the German statesman: 'The White Revolutionary: reflections on Bismarck'.[8] In his doctoral thesis, published as *A World Restored*, Kissinger focused on two other great figures of realism, Metternich and Castlereagh.[9] These two men – the first as foreign minister of the Austrian Empire and the second as British secretary of state for foreign affairs – were the architects of the balance of power more commonly known as the Concert of Europe, which held sway over the geopolitical order on the continent from 1815 to 1914.

More than fifteen years after he completed his thesis, the Concert of Europe would be an immense source of inspiration for Kissinger when orchestrating the rapprochement with Beijing and implementing the policy of Détente with the USSR. In normalising its diplomatic relations with the People's Republic of China, the United States would demonstrate that, just like the European powers in 1815, it would now be prepared to involve itself in a complex game of power balances, even if this meant rejecting the Manichaean paradigm setting Western democracies against Communist regimes whenever such a rejection was justified by America's interests. As regards Détente, it is tempting to imagine Kissinger relishing the idea that the Helsinki Conference was a new Congress of Vienna, with the collective security mechanisms representing his own contemporary version of the Concert of Europe.

Kissinger's interest in the system of the Congress of Vienna was also fed by his deep admiration for Metternich and Viscount

Realpolitik

Castlereagh. In Castlereagh (who killed himself in 1822), Kissinger saw a great statesman who, by laying the foundations of a lasting peace in Europe, enabled Great Britain to assert itself as the leading world power in the post-Napoleonic era. As US secretary of state, Kissinger sought to foster a similar equilibrium to preserve the interests and domination of the modern world's leading superpower.

But Castlereagh fascinated Kissinger for another reason. Hypersensitive to criticism, Henry could not fail to be touched by the tragic end of the man also known as Robert Stewart. Castlereagh had conceived and tirelessly promoted a style of British diplomacy steeped in realism because of his conviction that doing so would best preserve Britain's interests. But what his detractors saw as a form of *Realpolitik* earned him the scorn of the liberal British intelligentsia, who reproached his cynicism. Indeed, the romantic poet Lord Byron described Castlereagh brutally as an 'intellectual eunuch', a 'cold-blooded, smooth-fac'd, placid miscreant! (...) Cobbling at manacles for all mankind.'[10] Kissinger, who had a presentiment of the price he too would pay for being the architect of a realist American foreign policy, wrote: 'In every negotiation Castlereagh had to fight a more desperate battle with his Cabinet than with his foreign colleagues.'[11]

Kissinger's academic work led him to explore the Peace of Westphalia, which inspired the Concert of Europe. In bringing an end to the Thirty Years' War in 1648, the Peace of Westphalia marked a turning point in European history. For the first time, independent states agreed to abstain from interfering in the affairs of other states, thus recognising the existence of a balance of power on the continent. As Kissinger noted in admiration: 'The Westphalian peace reflected a practical accommodation to reality, not a unique moral insight.'[12]

We might take these words as a definition of realism according to Kissinger, as he attempted to pick his path between cynicism and idealism.

*

Henry Kissinger

Kissinger was in fact a realist in the most classical European tradition. He would undertake a rational, emotionless appraisal of current interests before coming up with an intentionally pragmatic policy. Kissingerian realism also posits the primacy of force as the foundation of credible diplomacy. As he himself wrote: 'Throughout history the political influence of nations has been roughly correlative to their military power.'[13] Without military power, any attempt to create a balance of power is doomed to failure because the mechanisms of deterrence no longer exist. Realism becomes nothing more than a form of cowardice in the face of mounting peril, as was the case with Neville Chamberlain in Munich.

Another component of Kissinger's realism was his rejection of any sort of ideology. As much as this put him on the same page as Nixon, it garnered the ire of the interventionist liberal left and neoconservatives. For the latter, the interests of American power must sometimes cede to moral imperatives, which could justify the United States pursuing crusades across the world. Henry, however, saw these 'moral crusades' as a dangerous manifestation of the art of the impossible, which he fought against.

However, it would be a major error to construe Kissinger's realism as amoral. As someone who had experienced the chaos of Nazi Germany and a Europe ripped apart by conflict, the ultimate moral aim of any foreign policy should be the avoidance of war by the establishment and preservation of a balance of power. During the Cold War, his primary goal was therefore to prevent a nuclear conflict between the two superpowers while preserving the United States' interests. If the realisation of this goal sometimes meant compromising important principles, then he accepted that, though without underestimating the consequences.

Kissinger had considerably more opportunity than many statesmen to reflect upon the moral consequences of his actions, owing to the academic work that preceded his exercise

Realpolitik

of foreign policy. He was aware that some of his decisions were likely to affect millions of people and lead to the deaths of innocents. But rather than bask in the kind of moralistic and idealistic diplomacy undertaken by the Carter administration, Kissinger was guided by an 'ethics of responsibility'.

The quest for a middle ground between, on the one hand, a foreign policy based solely on values and, on the other hand, a *Realpolitik* perceived as brutal and cynical, is what drove Kissinger's reflections and actions. Indeed, he was convinced that finding this shifting, fragile balance is what would make him a true statesman. As he explained in his writings, Metternich, Castlereagh and Bismarck could claim such a title because their political astuteness, their wisdom and their 'ability to recognize the real relationship of forces' allowed them to assuage anger and find a path that would prevent the world succumbing to a revolution synonymous with chaos.[14]

Between the end of the Napoleonic Wars and the age of the Cold War, the nature of the threat had changed. Nuclear weapons, which carry the risk of total destruction, had replaced conventional forms of warfare. But for Kissinger, nothing about the mission of a statesman had changed. It was the responsibility of the statesman to create the conditions for an equilibrium – as imperfect and unjust as it might be – capable of deterring any world power from provoking a new slide into chaos. For Metternich and Castlereagh, this chaos went by the name of Napoleon. For the Jewish child forced to flee his native land, this chaos would forever be personified by Hitler.

When he was in power, many commentators accused Kissinger of injecting a European strain of Machiavellianism into American foreign policy. As he noted with some irony: 'Americans are comfortable with an idealistic tradition that espouses great causes, such as making the world safe for democracy, or human rights.'[15] He felt, though, that their distrust of ambiguous compromises and their supposed natural inclination to frankness had not disposed them to building the alliances, as imperfect as they may be, necessary to the construction of a balance of power which, by definition, remains ever fragile and unstable.

The idealistic American tradition was chiefly embodied by the first United States secretary of state, Thomas Jefferson, as well as by Woodrow Wilson. The latter was convinced that national interests – by which Kissingerian realism is guided – could be transcended by the mechanisms of international law and multilateralism. But the American temptation to give in to the siren calls of idealism is also what led American diplomacy to seesaw between two extremes rejected by Kissinger: isolationism and interventionism.

It was not Kissinger, however, who introduced realism into American foreign policy. Jefferson's major rival, Alexander Hamilton, wrote: 'Safety from external danger is the most powerful director of national conduct.'[16] From the early nineteenth century, he expressed his refusal to believe in a natural harmony of interests between independent nation states. Then, less than a century later, Theodore Roosevelt and his secretary of state, John Hay, developed and implemented a diplomacy marked by realism, particularly in the brokering of an agreement to end the Russo-Japanese War and in the preservation of American interests regarding the Panama Canal.

Theodore Roosevelt and John Hay faced an issue that would also bother subsequent secretaries of state Henry Stimson, George Marshall and Dean Acheson: how to make their realism acceptable to the American people who, as Stanley Hoffmann would point out, remained 'traditionally hostile to balance of power diplomacy with its closets of partitions, compensations, secret treaties and gunboats'.[17] Rather than seeking to persuade their fellow citizens of the necessity to protect the interests of the United States, they masked their realism behind lyrical speeches lauding the special mission incumbent upon America. But seventy years later, the task would prove even harder for German-born Kissinger, suspected of wanting to import the

Realpolitik

cold and cynical calculations of European diplomacy into an America that fancied itself draped in a veil of purity.

Kissinger can only be described as a practitioner of *Realpolitik* if we adhere to August Ludwig von Rochau's original definition of the term. When he was in power, Kissinger was always trying to discern as clearly as possible the power plays, political manoeuvrings and motivations of the United States' allies and adversaries in order to develop and implement a foreign policy that would ensure a balance of power between Washington and Moscow. It was this balance of power that he saw as the only sustainable source of peace and the best means of preserving the interests of his adoptive country.

Kissinger was therefore a realist who tried to impose his vision of foreign policy on an American society that, while being no stranger to this way of thinking, never dared to accept it fully. A victim of this hypocrisy and of a liberal intelligentsia that made him its bête noire, Kissinger never stopped being the object of virulent attacks once he left office. Some were justified. His realism, which relied upon the primacy of the armed forces, sometimes led him to underestimate the importance of economic considerations and to ignore the growing role played by non-state actors. Nevertheless, these errors of analysis, albeit translated into questionable foreign policy choices, do not in themselves make Henry Kissinger an amoral figure.

In the nineteenth century, Viscount Castlereagh and Lord Palmerston, whose realist diplomacy enabled Great Britain to assert itself as the leading world power for more than a century, were also targets of their contemporaries' hatred and criticism. But as the decades passed and passions slowly cooled, history proved them right. Castlereagh and Palmerston are now considered among the greatest leaders that Britain has ever known. It is likely that Kissinger – so sensitive to the attacks made upon him – drew some comfort from the example of these two illustrious predecessors, whom he always held in the highest esteem.

Refugee

20 August 1938. As Heinz Kissinger turns to take a final look at Fürth, the town where he was born and grew up, he recalls the words of the father of his best friend, Menahem Lion, a few weeks before: 'You'll come back to your birthplace someday and you won't find a stone unturned.'[1]

His parents and his brother are with him. They have been able to bring only a few small pieces of furniture and a tiny sum of money. They can never have imagined that, less than three months later, their synagogue will be looted and destroyed as Kristallnacht rages across Germany.

Heinz is fifteen years old. He is now a refugee.

When Kissinger disembarked in New York, he tried to assimilate in every way, starting by asking to be called 'Henry' rather than Heinz. At George Washington High School, he worked extra hard to learn English almost from scratch. In the evenings, he would devour books on the history of the United States, as well as the great classics of American literature. Teenage Henry realised that education was the only way out if he wanted to be more than an impoverished refugee and become a fully integrated citizen of his adopted land. This was a common conviction among most German Jewish refugee families, but Henry demonstrated a seriousness and a maturity that set him apart from his peers.

Kissinger also quickly became a regular at Yankee Stadium, where he developed a passion for baseball. It was no accident that he set his heart on this sport, which embodies the American identity more than any other, transcending social classes.

His entire behaviour demonstrated what the historian Arthur Schlesinger – one of his closest friends – would call 'his refugee's desire for approval'.[2]

Gradually, he even managed to rid himself of the habit he had acquired as a child of crossing the street whenever a group of non-Jewish kids approached, to avoid being beaten up or called names. A few weeks after starting at high school, Henry was asked to write an essay about what it meant to be American. In it, he described his sadness at being separated from those he had spent his childhood with and the places he knew. But, he added, America was worth all these sacrifices and hardships because it was a country where you could hold your head up high as you walked down the street. And he concluded with a phrase that has bitter resonance in our current times, given how far the United States has drifted from this ideal over the past few years: 'our responsibility as Americans is always to make sure that our purposes transcend our differences'.[3]

Yet despite his thirst for integration, there were still many aspects of his everyday life that constantly reminded Kissinger of his German Jewish identity. First was his Bavarian accent, which he never managed to lose, however hard he tried. When he walked up the steps of his parents' building at the intersection of Fort Washington Avenue and 187th Street, it was not uncommon to hear only German voices, since many German Jewish families had found refuge in Washington Heights. This neighbourhood of northwest Manhattan – nicknamed the 'Fourth Reich' by New Yorkers – had the advantage of being cheap and full of synagogues, because of the successive waves of Jewish immigration from Poland and Russia.

At high school, Henry's classmates were all refugees. His only friends, with whom he went out in the evenings or headed up the Hudson Valley for weekend hikes, were Jews of German origin. His parents themselves socialised with nobody outside this circle. Indeed, Henry's father would often only leave the family apartment to go to synagogue with his son.

Refugee

It all drove Henry mad. Everything reminded him of this status of refugee that he so desperately wished to shake off.

In 1940, his excellent grades meant that he was accepted into the City College of New York without any difficulty. But there again, Henry was only following the trail already blazed by previous children of refugees. Still, he threw himself into his accountancy studies, but with little enthusiasm. His true dreams lay elsewhere.

The approaching war – the preliminary tremors of which had made him a refugee in the first place – was also the saving of him once it arrived. A few days before his nineteenth birthday, Kissinger received his call-up papers. Less than three months later, wearing the uniform of an infantryman, he found himself standing on the dusty drill square at Camp Croft in South Carolina. Here, on 19 June 1943, Henry Kissinger became an American citizen.

Henry's years in the army would mark a turning point in his life, as he bunked with Americans from all ethnic, religious and social backgrounds. Many of his comrades-in-arms came from the rural areas of Illinois, Wisconsin and Indiana. For the first time in his life, he was not surrounded only by German Jews. His humour and his maturity endeared him to the other soldiers, including some *rednecks* who had started out by making some antisemitic remarks to him. He also learned to appreciate the simplicity of these young men from the Midwest. A few years later, he even requested in his Harvard application to be given a roommate from this part of the United States.

But the army also allowed Kissinger to cease being a foreigner in his adopted country. Like hundreds of thousands of other immigrants, he would earn the honour of being American thanks to his courage at the front. No one would ever be able to cast doubts on his patriotism again. No one could dispute his right to feel as American as any young man born into a family who had lived on American soil for generations.

Henry Kissinger

When he crossed the German border, alone, on 9 November 1944, six years to the day after Kristallnacht, he was wearing an American uniform. There is something striking in the story of this young refugee who had to flee the country of his birth in fear and was now returning a conqueror. Yet Kissinger would never show any resentment about the German people. Even though the posts he held in the army gave him absolute power in denazifying certain German towns, including Bensheim, he made sure never to show any signs of hatred or vengeance.[4] When he saw an American soldier, a German Jewish refugee like him, abusively interrogating a civilian couple, he could not contain himself: 'You lived under the Nazis!' scolded Henry. 'You know how abusive they were! How can you turn around and abuse these people the same way?'[5]

Yet Kissinger was not ignorant of the horrors that had taken place following his family's departure for the United States. When he returned to Fürth for the first time, he couldn't help but think of what Menahem Lion's father had told him several years before. 'The Opera House, the culture house, the railroad station, the post office were all pounded into ruin,' Henry wrote in a letter to his parents. Determined to seek out his childhood friends, he quickly learned that, with one exception, all those who hadn't emigrated had been exterminated in the concentration camps. 'There on the hill overlooking Nuremberg,' he added, 'I said farewell to my youth.'[6]

When he returned to the United States and saw the New York skyline, Sergeant Kissinger no longer saw himself as a refugee, unlike the first time he'd seen that view. On that July day in 1947, he knew that America was now his nation and the country in which he would build his life. 'The army opened a new world for us,' his brother Walter would later say. 'One that our parents couldn't share or understand.'[7]

Over the previous three years, Henry had commanded men; he had survived war and it had toughened him up. Now he

Refugee

wanted to leave his past behind. But as much as he would often minimise the traumas of his youth when asked about them, they clearly stayed with him his whole life long.

Even as he ascended the ranks of power, he was haunted by a deep feeling of insecurity, which neither fame nor fortune could shift. Strolling the corridors of the White House, there was still a part of Henry that would always remain that young refugee boy from Washington Heights, nervous about not being liked or accepted for who he was.

This led him to desperately try to win over anyone who opposed him. He was more fascinated by his enemies than by his friends. This perverse mixture of arrogance and fragility was also what would make him so close to Nixon and feed his paranoia.

'Kissinger is a strong man, but the Nazis were able to damage his soul,' commented Fritz Kraemer, Henry's first mentor, who considered that the roots of his disciple's insecurity lay in his past as a refugee, and that his most salient personality traits could be traced to that experience. 'It made him seek order, and it led him to hunger for acceptance, even if it meant trying to please those he considered his intellectual inferiors.'[8]

Seen in this light, Kissinger's arrogance and vanity – so often described and condemned by his contemporaries – were simply the masks of a man plagued with the fear of being rejected. His compromises of principles and betrayals of his values were merely the consequence of his uncontrollable need for recognition. Kissinger would eventually grudgingly admit to this lack of confidence. 'Living as a Jew under the Nazis, then as a refugee in America, and then as a private in the army, isn't exactly an experience that builds confidence.'[9]

Rockefeller

Henry Kissinger felt almost dizzy as he walked into Nelson Rockefeller's thirty-two-room penthouse on Fifth Avenue for the first time. For this young man who had spent his childhood in a small house in Fürth and his late teenage years in a small apartment in the rundown Manhattan neighbourhood of Washington Heights, this residence embodied, more than any other place, that combination of power and social success to which he aspired.

As he wandered from room to room through this penthouse decorated by the famous French interior designer Jean-Michel Frank, Kissinger was dazzled by the masterpieces on display. Paintings by Degas and Picasso (including *Girl with a Mandolin*) hung alongside modern art pieces and African sculptures. In the large dining room, with its majestic mantelpieces, were two frescoes by Fernand Léger and Henri Matisse, while the furniture was designed by Alberto and Diego Giacometti.

As moved as Kissinger was by all these beautiful things, what fascinated him the most was the property's owner. Nelson Rockefeller was the king of New York, the flamboyant heir to one of America's largest fortunes – his grandfather had been one of the founders of Standard Oil. Courted by the most beautiful women and envied by the powerful, Rockefeller was an arts lover whose family philanthropy had earned him the presidency of the famous MoMA at barely thirty-one years of age.

One might think there would be an unbridgeable sociocultural abyss between the East Coast WASP (White Anglo-Saxon Protestant) patrician, whose charm was equalled only by his reputation as a dilettante, and the plump young Jewish refugee, ill at ease in social circles but whose intellect and capacity for work were already clearly exceptional. Yet their meeting in 1955 sparked a relationship that would prove decisive in Kissinger's life and career.

As he got to know his new mentor, the young Harvard doctoral student realised that if he wanted to scale the heights of power, then he absolutely needed to develop an aspect of his intelligence that he had neglected for far too long: human relations. Speaking about Rockefeller, Kissinger once said: 'He has a second-rate mind, but a first-rate intuition about people,' before adding: 'I have a first-rate mind, but a third-rate intuition about people.'[1]

Kissinger always knew that when it came to analytical capability and drawing conclusions, there would be very few people to rival him. But he now saw that he needed to learn how to flatter the ego and the vanity of those he was dealing with so as to be able to win them over and secure their trust. If, like many who were 'first in their class', he continued to ignore or even disdain that sort of intelligence, then his intellectual brio and capacity for work would not be enough for him to achieve his goal. What better model, then, than Rockefeller for him to learn how to master this art?

If Kissinger were a young man riddled with hang-ups, the same could not be said for his mentor. Nelson Rockefeller's self-confidence enabled him to see his own weaknesses clearly. He stuck to the precious advice his mother had once given him: 'Always surround yourself with people who are smarter than you.'

Just as he was always accompanied by stunning women, the New York billionaire drew the finest minds of his time into his inner circle. Among them Edward Teller, the father of the hydrogen bomb, and Dean Rusk, Lyndon B. Johnson's future secretary of state. He assigned them to task forces charged with producing recommendations that would expand his political vision.[2] Rockefeller cared little for the mockery of President Eisenhower, for example, who once remarked that he was 'too used to borrowing brains instead of using his own'.

Among this array of talents, Rockefeller very quickly spotted Kissinger. Joseph Persico, who was Rockefeller's speechwriter, commented that Henry possessed 'the combination of brilliance and egotism that Nelson always found entrancing'.[3]

In March 1956, a thirty-two-year-old Kissinger was appointed head of the Special Studies Project by Rockefeller. He had a hundred staff working under him and had to coordinate the work of several panels that included major figures from the political establishment and the business world. Kissinger took advantage of this to develop his network, considerably increasing his visibility in the circles of power, particularly after the publication of a report – which caused quite a buzz – aiming to be the theoretical response to the launch of Sputnik 1 by the Russians in October 1957.

Kissinger's new post allowed him to cement Rockefeller's trust in him, and he became the man's closest advisor. 'Rocky', as Nelson's supporters nicknamed him, asked Henry to draft his foreign policy speeches. The billionaire's entourage realised very soon, however, that although the young Harvard academic was undoubtedly gifted, handling his huge ego would prove to be a most delicate task.

For example, Kissinger noticed one day that a speech he had written for his boss had been slightly altered by Rockefeller's team of writers. He stormed into their office in fury and yelled: 'When Nelson buys a Picasso, he does not hire four house painters to improve it.' From that day forth, the writing team started calling themselves 'the house painters'.[4]

Despite the tensions between Kissinger and the rest of the staff, relations between Rockefeller and Kissinger only grew stronger.

Even after he left New York in autumn 1957 to return to his

academic career at Harvard, Kissinger continued to work as a consultant to his mentor, something that would only end when he entered the White House in January 1969. Indeed, the total fees paid to him by Rockefeller reveal that Kissinger's work for his 'boss' was particularly intense in 1960, 1964 and 1968; years that, unsurprisingly, coincide with Rockefeller's three attempts to win the Republican primaries.

Rocky's initial political successes had led him to harbour much bigger national ambitions. Rockefeller would serve a total of four successive terms as governor of the State of New York, having first been elected in 1959. His charm worked just as effectively on both the most powerful and the lowliest of his compatriots. His natural ease with people allowed him to forge an authentic bond with voters despite his extremely privileged origins.

Asked by the *Atlantic* in 2016 about the greatest politician he had ever had the opportunity to meet, Kissinger paid homage to the talent of Nelson Rockefeller, mentioning him alongside Ronald Reagan and Bill Clinton.[5] But unlike Reagan and Clinton, who had also started their political careers as governors, Rockefeller never attained the national office he dreamed of. His social conscience and his centrism, which New Yorkers appreciated so much, alienated him from the Republican base. The post of vice president to Gerald Ford, which he held briefly and unremarkably from 1974 to 1977, made no difference whatsoever.

So strong was the personal relationship that Kissinger developed with Rockefeller over the course of the fourteen years he spent working for him that it was a huge surprise for the whole Rockefeller team when Henry accepted Nixon's offer of the prestigious post of national security advisor at the White House. He was quickly accused of treachery.

Everyone knew that by enlisting Kissinger's services, Nixon was trying to overcome a complex he had always had about his

Republican rival. Even once he was ensconced in the White House, Nixon was tormented by the idea that he would never have either the wealth or the charm of Nelson Rockefeller. Drawing Kissinger into his web meant swiping the jewel in the crown of the man he so envied.

Yet there was one person from whom Kissinger received zero grief regarding his appointment, and that person was Nelson Rockefeller. As Kissinger tentatively asked his mentor if he should accept the post, Rocky began by reproving him for playing hard-to-get with the president-elect. 'You have no right to treat a president that way,' he admonished. Then he added: 'Henry, have you ever considered that Nixon is taking a bigger risk on you than you are on him?' This conversation sealed Kissinger's decision.[6]

But even while working for Nixon, Kissinger never broke off links with Rockefeller. He who so readily criticised anyone who crossed his path remained perfectly loyal to his former boss, something which Nixon bitterly resented. 'He knew that Rockefeller and I had been rivals for years,' Nixon lamented one day. 'If he had wanted to pander to me, he could on occasion have said something critical of Rockefeller.'[7]

Following Rockefeller's funeral on 29 January 1979, during which he could barely hold back his tears, Kissinger was one of the few of Nelson's inner circle to be invited back for the reception held at Kykuit, the family estate acquired by the patriarch, John D. Rockefeller, in 1893. From the grand house overlooking the Hudson River, he could make out the New York City skyline on the horizon. For the space of a few moments, the entirety of the past twenty-four years since he had first met Nelson Rockefeller came flashing back to him. He knew that without Rocky he would never have had the career that he did.

Henry also recalled the words that his mentor had spoken to him one May evening in 1973 when Kissinger was celebrating his fiftieth birthday at the Colony Club on Park Avenue,

Henry Kissinger

surrounded by his dearest friends. In the course of the dinner, Nelson Rockefeller gave a toast in honour of his friend that touched Henry deeply. 'There's always been the question of whether history makes the man or the man makes history. Henry has settled the question. The man has made history.'[8]

Sadat

When Anwar Sadat became the new president of Egypt on 15 October 1970, Henry Kissinger didn't hide his scorn for the man. Talking to Golda Meir, he described Gamal Abdel Nasser's successor as: 'a fool, a clown, a buffoon'[1] – an opinion of the new leader that many people shared.

Sadat, who described himself in his autobiography as 'a peasant born and brought up on the banks of the Nile',[2] indeed had neither the charisma of his predecessor nor the wiliness of Hafez al-Assad. Conspiratorial, a tactician rather than a strategist, he owed his political ascent only to the constant protection of Nasser. The pair met in 1938 and had taken part together in the coup that helped topple King Farouk I in 1952, following which Sadat held a series of prestigious posts but without any real power. When Nasser died of a heart attack, many observers felt that Sadat was only a transitional leader whose days at the head of the country were numbered.

The Egyptian people themselves had little respect for this apparatchik with his dark skin (inherited from his Sudanese mother) and refined suits. There was a popular Egyptian quip: 'Golda Meir may scare us to death, but Anwar Sadat makes us die laughing.' The new president raged about not being taken seriously, particularly since he was also underestimated by the Soviets who, over the course of Nasser's supreme domination of Egypt, had progressively cemented their influence in the country and were now convinced that Sadat would be content to serve as a docile and obedient puppet while they looked for a successor more to their liking. Indeed, Leonid Brezhnev treated Sadat with disdain during his two visits to Moscow in early

1972. And the Americans – particularly Kissinger – paid scant attention to what they saw as a bland figure bleating on about a war against Israel.

In a speech given on 4 May 2000 at the University of Maryland, Kissinger admitted as much: 'I am quite frank to say that I did not understand Anwar Sadat when he first became president. Our intelligence reports described him as a weak man (...). Everyone expected two or three other leaders of Egypt to overthrow him at any moment. And Anwar Sadat made many threats, many statements, none of which, to my shame I must say, I took very seriously. Because it was absolutely axiomatic with us that there was no conceivable way that Egypt would dare to start a war.'[3]

From the start of his presidency, Sadat was well aware of all the criticisms and the jibes. But deep down, there was a rock-solid self-confidence he ascribed to his village upbringing built on 'fraternity, cooperation, and love'. As he wrote in his autobiography, this happy childhood 'deepened my feeling of inner superiority, a feeling which has never left me and which, I came to realize in time, is an inner power independent of all material resources'.[4]

In spring 1971, as rumours of a coup d'état spread, Sadat decided to strike hard. Numerous army and special forces officers were rounded up. A few months later, with the military establishment now brought into line, he had two of the regime's most powerful figures arrested and thrown in jail: the vice president Ali Sabri, who had close relations with the Soviets, and the minister of interior, Sharawi Gomaa, who controlled the much-feared secret police.

Imagine the Kremlin's surprise when, barely a month later, in July 1972, Sadat ordered the immediate expulsion of the 25,000 Soviet military advisors stationed in Egypt. 'I wanted to tell the whole world that we are always our own masters,' he would explain.[5]

Above all, although he officially adhered to Nasserist

ideology, Sadat was convinced that the moment had come for Egypt to close the book on the socialist era and take a more free-market turn. He wished to sow the seeds of a future alliance with the United States, an alliance he now judged essential for his country. Fascinated by American power, Sadat was certain that it was in Washington that the future of the Middle East would play out.

But despite such demonstrative gestures from the Egyptian president and the secret meetings that Henry and Hafez Ismail (nicknamed the 'Kissinger of Egypt')[6] had had in New York, Nixon's national security advisor still paid Sadat little mind – being preoccupied with the war in Vietnam, Détente with the USSR and the policy of rapprochement with Beijing. And although he had watched with satisfaction the repeated failures of Secretary of State William Rogers to resolve the Arab-Israeli conflict, he had hitherto taken pains to avoid engaging with this dossier. To the Arab leaders who urged him to focus more on the subject, Kissinger replied: 'I will never get involved in anything unless I'm sure of success. And if I do get involved it means I'm going to succeed. I hate failure.' Then, he added: 'The Middle East isn't ready for me.'[7]

Events, however, would not afford Kissinger the luxury of indulging in such arrogant declarations much longer.

On 6 October 1973, at dawn, Sadat launched an all-out attack on Israel, in concertation with Syria, putting the Israelis on the back foot on two fronts. Alerted in the middle of the night, Kissinger called Sadat a 'madman', assuming that, just as during the Six-Day War of 1967, the IDF would quickly crush the Arab armies. He fast realised, however, that Israel was in a critical situation.

This attack on the day of Yom Kippur, when many Israeli soldiers were on leave, was, to quote the Israeli foreign minister Abba Eban, 'a second Pearl Harbor'. The Syrians made rapid advances over the Golan Heights, while the Egyptians crossed the Suez Canal and breached the Bar-Lev Line. In the Egyptian parliament, Sadat declared: 'We have always felt the sympathy of the world but we would prefer the respect of the world to sympathy without respect.'[8]

Kissinger found himself at the controls, Nixon being somewhat absent because of the fallout from the Watergate scandal. And so the man who had taken the oath of office as secretary of state only two weeks before, now had the delicate task of saving Israel from a defeat that might prove fatal.

After a very tricky few days, the Israeli troops, with American logistical support, managed to launch a counter-offensive and emerge victorious. Soon the city of Suez was being besieged by the IDF, while to the southwest of the canal, the Egyptian Third Army was encircled. A ceasefire was decreed, but the belligerents stood their ground, and it looked as if hostilities could break out again at any moment.

So Kissinger decided to play the role of mediator between Golda Meir, who travelled to Washington, and the Egyptian foreign minister, Ismail Fahmi, whom Sadat dispatched to the American capital. From the start of the war the Egyptian president had made it known to Kissinger that he was ready to negotiate. Indeed, his reason for attacking Israel had been to manoeuvre to a position where he could achieve a peace agreement that he knew was impossible without the involvement of the United States. He had also come to the conclusion that no peace agreement worthy of the name could be envisaged in the Middle East as long as Israel considered that its military superiority was the sole guarantor of its security. Golda Meir hadn't been mistaken when, in 1970, she had seen in the Egyptian president a 'reasonable man who might soberly consider the benefits' of a lasting peace with Israel.[9] What she had not anticipated, however, was the method he would employ to achieve his goal.

Despite the Israeli counterattack, Sadat's bet paid off. Arab pride was restored following the humiliation of 1967. The

Egyptian people now viewed their leader as a hero who had restored their country's honour. Sadat knew full well that he would never be capable of beating the IDF militarily, but his surprise attack had earned him the prestige and the necessary political weight to reach a negotiated settlement.

This was the background to the first meeting between Kissinger and Sadat, on 7 November 1973, in Cairo. The two men talked for over three hours, each trying to outcharm the other. Sadat proved particularly gifted at this game, having dreamed of becoming an actor in his youth and harbouring an attraction for the theatre all his life. Kissinger was enthralled and realised quite how mistaken his previous judgements had been.

In his memoirs, the former secretary of state commented: 'From that meeting onward, I knew I was dealing with a great man.'[10] Then, to emphasise all the respect and admiration he had for the Egyptian leader, he wrote: 'The great man understands the essence of a problem; the ordinary leader grasps only the symptoms. The great man focuses on the relationship of events to each other; the ordinary leader sees only a series of seemingly disconnected events. The great man has a vision of the future that enables him to put obstacles in perspective; the ordinary leader turns pebbles in the road into boulders.'[11]

The attraction was mutual. Sadat was impressed by Kissinger's exceptional intelligence. In his autobiography, he covered this meeting in detail. 'For the first time, I felt as if I was looking at the real face of the United States, the one I had always wanted to see – not the face put on by Dulles, Dean Rusk, and Rogers. Anyone seeing us after that first hour in al-Tahrah Palace would have thought we had been friends for years.'[12]

Just as he did with Zhou Enlai, Henry particularly admired the sense of history that fed Sadat's reflections. As he would say later: 'Sadat had the wisdom to understand that a fundamental change was necessary. He also represented a country with a deep intuition for eternity through a long history surpassing that of Arab states created after the Treaty of Versailles.'[13]

In the course of their meeting, the two men agreed a six-point plan, which would serve as a basis for negotiations with the Israelis. But above all, the meeting marked the starting point of a unique relationship that would lead to a peace process and change the course of the Middle East. They also agreed to re-establish diplomatic relations between Cairo and Washington (broken off in 1967), a great victory for both of them.

Kissinger had managed to coax one of the major Middle East powers out of the Soviet orbit, a power that had always offered unconditional support to Moscow ever since Nasser's takeover. And in forging this alliance with Egypt, he became the first American high official to lay the foundations of a true 'Arab policy'. As for Sadat, he had succeeded in defying the Kremlin and turning his back on Arab socialism to create the conditions for a special relationship with the United States. He knew that American aid, both economic and military, was now indispensable to him, both at home and abroad. As he explained in an interview given to the Egyptian magazine *Rose al-Youssef*: 'Before the October War, the United States didn't even hear us. But Egyptian soldiers crossed the canal and demolished the Bar-Lev Line, upending the established view of Israel's security, and the United States realised the threats to their oil interests. It forced them to reassess their policy. We must take advantage of it.'[14]

The blossoming relationship between Egypt and the United States led to Nixon's triumphal visit to Cairo in June 1974. A little over a year later, in October 1975, under the presidency of Gerald Ford, Sadat became the first Egyptian president to undertake a state visit to the United States. The man who orchestrated both historic meetings was none other than Kissinger.

But the secretary of state did not stop there. He felt that the Middle East was now 'ready' for him. Although the Israelis and Egyptians had undertaken to respect the ceasefire for the time being, he knew that he had to broker a disengagement agreement between Cairo and Jerusalem. After a flurry of meetings with Golda Meir and Sadat in late 1973, January 1974 saw Kissinger commence a frenetic bout of what the media called 'shuttle diplomacy'.

Accompanied by several officials handpicked for their talents – including Harold H. Saunders, the Middle East expert on the National Security Council, and Roy Atherton of the State Department – Kissinger shuttled back and forth between Jerusalem and Aswan, where the president liked to spend some of the winter. There wasn't a moment of respite for the secretary of state and his team. They would leave the New Cataract hotel in Aswan in the early hours and spend the first part of the morning negotiating the terms of an agreement with Sadat. Then they would fly to Jerusalem to continue discussions with Golda Meir. Meetings could last five or six hours. Some days, they would fly back and forth several times. Time spent in the plane gave Kissinger and his team the chance to get their notes in order, think about the right tactic to adopt and keep President Nixon and Vice President Ford up to date. If he felt it was necessary, Kissinger would take a quick flight to Riyad, Algiers or another Arab capital to talk directly with the leaders of the region.

According to Saunders, their plane became a veritable mobile office. Kissinger was constantly asking his staff to update and annotate the checklists he took with him into each negotiation. One day, as they were preparing to land at an Egyptian military base, Henry flew into a rage because the latest version of a document wasn't ready. Once the plane had touched down, the pilot was ordered to keep on taxiing until this document was finalised. For ten minutes, the American plane rolled up and down the runway under the bemused gaze of the Egyptian foreign minister waiting on the sweltering tarmac.[15]

But these efforts did bear fruit, and on 18 January 1974, a disengagement treaty was signed between the Israelis and the Egyptians at Kilometre 101 of the road between Cairo and Suez.

Israel agreed to pull back to around twenty kilometres from the Suez Canal, with a buffer zone created between the two armies. This was the first step towards a lasting peace between these two nations hitherto riven by what Sadat once described as 'a gulf of bad blood, violence and massacres'.[16]

Kissinger didn't believe it was possible in the near future to achieve a global peace agreement in the Middle East. He considered it to be an unrealistic aim and instead focused on step-by-step diplomacy. The secretary of state saw the peace process as a series of interim accords contributing to a wider political process. He was convinced that in this particular region, more than anywhere else, history could only be made through gradual steps.

In spring 1974, Kissinger resumed his shuttle diplomacy, this time between Damascus and Jerusalem. At the end of a diplomatic marathon lasting thirty-three days, he succeeded in finding the key to an accord that put an end to the war of attrition that had continued to rumble on since the ceasefire was agreed. On 10 June 1974, *TIME* magazine put Kissinger on the cover with the title 'Mideast Miracle'.[17] It is fair to say that, more than any other moment in his career, this was the period that saw Kissinger deploy his negotiating talents and formidable resilience with the most exceptional brio. What was especially tricky for Kissinger in these step-by-step negotiations was that he was dealing with counterparts who had quite different characters. He described Hafez al-Assad as the master of the 'salami slicing' tactic, which involves putting an extreme position on the table, then, as the negotiations gradually progress, 'slicing' the salami a little at a time – making small concessions as you move towards agreement. Sadat, on the other hand, was a leader whose approach was to 'state a great objective and not haggle over every detail'. What Kissinger most respected in Sadat was that he didn't seek to please his subordinates, but rather 'to look good to history'.[18]

This shuttle diplomacy was not always crowned with success, however. Following intense negotiations with King Hussein of Jordan, in summer and autumn 1974, the master of American diplomacy understood that, in light of the pressure put on the Hashemite Kingdom by other Arab capitals, he would not be able to seal a deal between Jerusalem and Amman.

So in September 1975, it was once again with Sadat, who never missed an opportunity to refer to him in public as 'my friend', that Kissinger managed to conclude a new Egypt–Israel agreement, following an initial attempt back in March. Under the terms of this Sinai Interim Agreement, signed on 4 September 1975 in Geneva, Israel would return the oil fields of the Gulf of Suez to Egypt and withdraw further to the eastern ends of the Mitla and Gidi passes in the mountains of the Sinai. Above all, Israel and Egypt agreed that 'the conflict between them and in the Middle East shall not be resolved by military force but by peaceful means'.[19]

One of the more fascinating aspects of the friendship between Kissinger and Sadat was the way it helped to increase the prestige of both exceptional men. Their special relationship, built of mutual trust and admiration, led them to take risks and free them of the straitjackets within which they might so easily have remained trapped. We should not underestimate the disagreements, threats and hatred that both men faced, Sadat in particular.

Many Arab leaders looked most unfavourably upon the peace initiatives that the Egyptian president was pursuing. In an effort to ramp up the pressure on Sadat, the Saudis decided to suspend their considerable economic and military aid to Cairo. Having been feted as a hero after the Yom Kippur War, Anwar Sadat was now seen by a significant proportion of Arab public opinion as the man who betrayed the Palestinian cause. The threats to his life became deadlier. In 1975, after receiving a tip-off from Israeli intelligence, Kissinger alerted his friend that the Iraqi regime was out to assassinate him.

But Sadat did not give in to fear. 'I am Egyptian first, Arab second,' he would say. After all, he knew full well that it was his own Egyptian people who had paid dearly in blood over the successive Arab–Israeli wars. He had nothing but scorn for those leaders who blamed him for rupturing Arab unity. He refused to allow that his nation remain a martyr for the Palestinian cause much longer, a cause that the other countries of the region used to salve their conscience.

As for Kissinger, he did not hesitate to push the Israeli leadership into a corner. In 1975, he sensed that the Jewish State, now led by Yitzhak Rabin, was less than eager to negotiate a new agreement with Egypt. So the secretary of state decided to put maximum pressure on Israel. While he never called into question the strength of the alliance between Jerusalem and Washington, Kissinger was convinced that things could only progress in the Middle East if the United States showed itself to be dealing firmly with its ally. Few American statesmen thought this. Even fewer put it into action. It earned Kissinger some acerbic criticism from a portion of the American Jewish electorate. But like Sadat, he understood that there was no other path to peace.

The relationship forged by Sadat and Kissinger therefore marked the start of, and created the conditions for, a peace process that would continue long after Kissinger had left office. What followed – the Egyptian president's historic visit to Jerusalem in 1977, the awarding of the Nobel Peace Prize jointly to Anwar Sadat and the Israeli prime minister Menachem Begin in 1978, as well as the Camp David Accords, which would lead to the Egypt–Israel Peace Treaty of 1979 – would never have been possible without the efforts of two men who were prepared to do anything to ensure that diplomacy won out over prejudices and traditional mindsets.

During his future visits to the United States, Sadat, of whom Kissinger would write that he 'had the wisdom and courage of the statesman and occasionally the insight of the prophet',[20] would always try to find time for his 'friend'. In August 1981, having just met President Reagan, Sadat invited Henry to join him on the flight from Washington to New York. 'You know, next March,' he announced with enthusiasm, 'the Sinai is coming back to us. It's going to be a big celebration. And since you and I started this, you should come to Egypt and celebrate with us.' Sensing the slight embarrassment of his friend, the Egyptian president paused. Then, he said: 'No, you're Jewish. It is very painful for the Israelis to give up this territory. And if they see you in Cairo celebrating with us, they'll be very hurt and we mustn't do this to them. I have a better idea.' His eyes gleaming with joy, he looked at Henry and told him: 'Let the territory come back. And then, a month later, you and I alone will take a trip through the Sinai and we'll go to the top of Mount Sinai where I intend to build a synagogue, a mosque and a church. And this will be a more meaningful celebration of the peace process than if you come to Cairo.'[21]

This dream would never come to pass. On 6 October 1981, barely two months after that conversation, Anwar Sadat was assassinated in Cairo.

Teacher

The French philosopher and political scientist Raymond Aron was a great connoisseur of the United States and was always keen to forge new intellectual and political connections at the country's highest levels. It was during one of his many transatlantic visits that he made the acquaintance of Henry Kissinger. Aron had come to talk with John Fitzgerald Kennedy, then 'merely' the senator for Massachusetts. Several of his friends suggested he also meet a young and ambitious Harvard academic who, like Aron, seemed unwilling to confine himself to academia and showed a pronounced taste for politics.

Their meeting in 1957 marked the beginning of a wonderful friendship that would endure until Aron's death in 1983. Although Kissinger was only just beginning his academic career, Aron agreed to write three pieces for *Confluence*, the journal which his young American peer had recently launched with a view to cementing his reputation in the field of international relations. In 1962, it was Raymond Aron's turn to convince his friend to open a centre for European studies at Harvard. It still exists. For the past thirty-five years, this centre has been based in one of the most stunning buildings in Cambridge, Massachusetts – Adolphus Busch Hall – which stands out from the rest of the campus because of its Germanic architecture.

The friendship linking Aron and Kissinger was not immune to deep disagreements, particularly after Kissinger took over the reins of American diplomacy. The close relationship between the two men would, however, always be one of great mutual esteem.

In his *Memoirs*, Raymond Aron emphasises that Kissinger

never made him feel 'the sense of his intellectual superiority which he is said to inflict on mere mortals'.[1] As for the American diplomat, he considered that 'Aron was the only one with whom I could have a meaningful discussion'.[2] Indeed Kissinger penned the dedication 'To my teacher' in the copy of his own memoirs that he gave to Aron. In 1984, Kissinger again referred to the author of *The Opium of the Intellectuals* as his 'teacher' in the double issue of *Commentaire* devoted to Aron's work.[3] Six years later, he used the same term in his introduction to the English translation of Aron's *Memoirs*.[4]

Beyond their sometimes diverging opinions, there was one other key difference between Aron and Kissinger. Unlike his American friend, Aron never acceded to any position of political responsibility.

Keeping a distance from the political realm allowed Aron to maintain an intellectual independence and a liberty of tone, to which he was deeply attached. Crossing the political Rubicon would have risked sullying a reputation built up over many years, and would have obliged him to make his peace with certain intellectual constructions or, worse, compromise his moral principles.

Yet Aron could not but observe, with a mixture of fascination and envy, his American counterpart as he outlined and directed the diplomacy of the world's leading superpower. The French intellectual saw his work in no other terms than being intrinsically linked to political debate.

As Jean d'Ormesson wrote in his autobiographical work *Le vagabond qui passe sous une ombrelle trouée*: 'Raymond Aron (...) was the first to express his surprise at not having been the French Kissinger,' before adding, apropos of this man he knew so well: 'Let me be quite clear: had I been de Gaulle, Pompidou or Giscard [d'Estaing], I would have picked Aron as my "Prince's advisor".'[5]

*

As vastly different as their career paths may have been, Kissinger and Aron shared a deep distrust of trite concepts that claim to explain the complexity of diplomatic-strategic conduct. Born European, Kissinger was much closer to his French friend in this regard than he was to the American theoreticians of international relations who frequently failed to take the trouble to subject their concepts to history's unforgiving critique.

In his *Études politiques*, published in 1972, Aron wrote that, on the contrary: 'The course of international relations remains supremely historical, in every sense of this term: changes are incessant; the systems, diverse and fragile, are subject to the repercussions of every economic, technical or moral transformation; decisions taken by one or a handful of men set in motion millions of men and trigger irreversible mutations, with infinitely lingering consequences.'[6] Kissinger could have written those very same lines.

Despite their intellectual proximity, Aron had no hesitation in proffering vehement criticism of certain aspects of his friend's diplomacy. His editorials in *Le Figaro*, as well as his correspondence with Kissinger, were the two primary means by which Aron expressed his disagreements.

The French philosopher was a fervent critic of the policy of Détente implemented by Kissinger. He saw in it the formal recognition of an American–Soviet condominium, which could only be to the detriment of the Europeans. In particular, he feared that the attainment of a balance of power between the US and the USSR would result in the 'Finlandisation' of Europe. His fears were even greater, given that, as he so lucidly explained: 'If the Western Europeans were to find themselves in a situation comparable to that of the Finns, I doubt that they would display the same courage and retain a similar share of liberty.'[7]

Writing a dispatch for *Le Figaro* from the Helsinki conference (a symbol of this policy of Détente), Aron opined that, unlike the Congress of Vienna, Helsinki would not lead to a new order that ensured the stability of Europe. Rather, it would rubber-stamp faits accomplis: 'the states participating in the conference did not concur on the principle of legitimacy but on the carving up of Europe between incompatible principles'.[8]

Aron's disagreements with Kissinger were primarily those of a European. Behind their different views of Détente lay the consequences of their diverging personal choices. Kissinger, who had grown up a German Jew, had become an American. Aron, born into a Jewish family, had chosen to remain French, despite the depravities of history. The building of a political Europe was a dream that he had never had to give up. Conversely, as the master of American diplomacy, Kissinger could no longer be the defender of this ambition, which, in many ways, appeared to him incompatible with certain interests of his adoptive country.

But it was also ethical considerations that brought the two men to loggerheads. Revolted by the Nixon administration's abandoning of South Vietnam,[9] followed by their support of the coup d'état in Chile in September 1973, Aron did not mince his words in criticising the United States. The roots of this critique did not lie in any sympathy for the socialist experiment pursued by Salvador Allende. Unlike the vast majority of the French intelligentsia, he was clear-eyed as regards the Chilean president's faults, and he knew that the errors of the Popular Unity government had plunged Chile into something approaching civil war. But for Aron, nothing could justify a military coup and the use of violence against a democratically elected government.[10]

His criticisms were even more strident because he feared, and rightly so, that the sort of American interventions seen in Latin America might be repeated on European soil. As was often the case with Aron, events very quickly proved him right. His dark predictions became a reality when a military coup, supported by the CIA, occurred in Cyprus on 15 July 1974, toppling the president of the Republic of Cyprus, Archbishop Makarios III – nicknamed the 'Fidel Castro of the eastern Mediterranean' by the American press.

On 19 September 1974, Aron wrote his friend a long letter. In it, he condemned in no uncertain terms the diplomacy pursued by the man who was now the secretary of state:

> Must the United States, owing to its global responsibilities, never take moral stands, never approve or blame other than for pragmatic reasons? (...) A dominant power such as the United States must also embody ideas. (...) When we were both professors, we discussed the difficulties of marking out the boundaries between realism and cynicism. You have other fish to fry than to philosophise. But you believe, as I do, that, at a certain level, creative action goes hand in hand with a philosophy.[11]

For many years, first as a student and then as an academic, Kissinger, like Aron, had attempted to theorise a realist foreign policy. But now that Kissinger found himself in the position to implement it, his French friend reproached him for divorcing it from any morals. For Aron, the disdain for democratic ideals carried within it the seeds of failure; any foreign policy informed by such a disdain would be ultimately unrealistic. Leaving aside the essentially divergent interests of Aron the European and Kissinger the American, this was the only true point of disagreement – but oh, what an important one – between these two intellectual giants.

Zhou Enlai

M.F.H. Beg was in a crabby mood as his plane landed in Islamabad in the early hours of 9 July 1971. 'The fact is', he said to himself, 'my career as a stringer is going nowhere. I spend my time researching stories out in the sticks of Pakistan and writing them up, only for no one to publish them. My life's just passing me by.' As he was stepping onto the tarmac, Beg noticed several Western types walking quickly towards a private plane. He couldn't believe his eyes: the serious demeanour, the gait. Could it be? Yes, it was! The man in the middle of the bunch was none other than Henry Kissinger.

Beg homed in on the nearest police officer, who was watching the scene. 'Where's that plane going?' he asked. 'Beijing,' the guy answered. 'Beijing! But that's not possible. Are you sure?' 'Yes. In fact, the pilots of the plane are themselves Chinese,' replied the officer, who had no idea of the value of the information he had just provided.

His heart beating fast, Beg dashed to the first payphone he could find in Islamabad airport. 'Pass me the editor-in-chief of the *Daily Telegraph*!' he yelled at the switchboard operator who took his call. 'I must speak with him as a matter of urgency!' A few moments later, an aggravated voice came on the line: 'What is so important to wake me up in the middle of the night?' Beg took his courage in both hands. 'I know you're going to find this hard to believe, but I just saw Henry Kissinger at Islamabad airport. I even have confirmation that he is about to fly to Beijing!' A silence followed, only a few seconds, but it seemed to Beg like an eternity. Then, the editor-in-chief lost his temper: 'What on earth are you on about? The *New York Times*, and all the major papers, report that Kissinger is currently resting up in Nathia Gali in Northern Pakistan because of some stomach ailment. What would he be going to Beijing for? The United States has not had diplomatic relations with China for more than twenty years.'

Beg implored him: 'Sir, I swear it was Kissinger.' 'Enough!' the editor-in-chief cut him off. 'One more word and I'll terminate your contract with the *Daily Telegraph*. We are a serious newspaper, so spare me your nonsense! And a bit of advice, Beg: sort out your drinking problem. It'll stop you making a monkey of yourself in future.' With these last words, the editor-in-chief of the *Daily Telegraph* hung up. Beg had just seen his scoop of the century kicked into touch. And Kissinger, without knowing it, had had fortune smile on him at a crucial moment.[1]

Contrary to the official communiqué issued by the White House and published by the most important newspapers in the world, Kissinger had never stopped in Nathia Gali to rest. The motorcade awaiting him outside a local airstrip was there only for show. The national security advisor had in fact travelled directly to Islamabad in order to fly on to China in the greatest secrecy. Beg had been right. But what the Pakistani journalist didn't know was that this secret flight of Kissinger's would change the world.

A few hours later, a little after noon, Henry Kissinger set foot on Chinese soil for the first time in his life, accompanied by just three colleagues and two Secret Service agents. He was whisked off to Diaoyutai State Guesthouse in the heart of the Chinese capital. It was here, beside a little lake, surrounded by a huge park, that he would meet Zhou Enlai. Zhou was the loyal right-hand man of Mao Zedong and had been the premier of the People's Republic of China since its proclamation on 1 October 1949.

Kissinger was conscious, however, that he faced an initial obstacle. During the 1954 Geneva Conference, which settled a number of issues relating to the Korean Peninsula after the end of the First Indochina War, the then secretary of state, John Foster Dulles, had refused to shake Zhou Enlai's hand. This gesture (or rather the lack of it) was felt by the Chinese to be a deep humiliation. Kissinger knew that this wound had not healed despite the passing of seventeen years. He would have to convince the Chinese leader that such an affront would never occur again.

As soon as the Chinese Premier entered, Kissinger ostentatiously stuck out his hand. For a moment, he wondered if Zhou Enlai would make him pay the price for the past affront. On the contrary. The handshake that followed marked the start of a personal relationship, the strength of which would profoundly influence Sino–American relations. 'It was the first step in putting the legacy of the past behind us,' Kissinger would later state.[2]

Over the next two days, Zhou and Kissinger spoke for more than seventeen hours. The American diplomat was fascinated by the Chinese leader's charisma and intelligence. Kissinger described these talks as 'the most searching, sweeping and significant discussions I have ever had in government'.[3]

To gain Zhou's trust, Kissinger showed him confidential information collected by the American intelligence services about Soviet military installations on the Chinese–Russian border. Henry knew full well that the Chinese premier, along with the principal officials of the regime, was deeply mistrustful of Moscow.

Zhou very quickly gave his consent to what was the prime objective of Kissinger's trip: have the Chinese authorities extend an invitation to Nixon for an official visit to Beijing in early 1972. A communiqué, the content of which would remain secret, stated that 'having been appraised of President Nixon's desire to visit the People's Republic of China', he was invited with a view to 'normalising relations' between the two powers.

The thorny issue of Taiwan was carefully avoided. Kissinger then informed the White House of his success by a coded message one word long: 'Eureka.'

Their mission accomplished, Kissinger and Zhou entered into long discussions on the global balance of powers. The two men were drawn together by a shared love of history and big ideas. Indeed, Henry would comment that their exchange was like 'a dialogue between two professors of political philosophy'. Of Zhou, Kissinger wrote: 'He was equally at home in philosophy, reminiscence, historical analysis, tactical probes, humorous repartee.'[4] He saw in the man who had exercised a certain restraint on Mao's excesses – so alleviating his people's suffering, notably during the Great Leap Forward and the Cultural Revolution – the embodiment of the Confucian mandarin. He noted that Zhou had an 'exceptional intelligence and capacity to intuit the intangibles of the psychology of his opposite number'.[5]

For the Chinese people, Zhou remains the most loved Chinese leader of the twentieth century, even today. The image of the sage, so closely associated with him, was nourished by an episode that occurred during Nixon's historic visit to China from 21 to 28 February 1972. To the president's question about how he viewed the French Revolution, Zhou Enlai replied that it was 'still too early to say'. When this exchange was made public, many saw it as an illustration of the Chinese leadership's long-term thinking, whereas Western leaders too often gave in to the diktats of short-termism. Of course, this anecdote was too good to be true. Forty years later, Chas Freeman, the American interpreter present for the meeting, explained that Zhou's answer referred not to the revolution of 1789 but to the events of May 1968. This was, as Freeman put it himself, 'a misunderstanding that was too delicious to invite correction'.[6]

This takes nothing away from the fascination that Zhou Enlai exercised over Kissinger, who considered him, along with de Gaulle and Sadat, as 'one of the two or three most impressive men I have ever met'.[7]

From their very first meeting, Kissinger was struck, not by his physical presence, but by the mixture of grace and serenity that Zhou exuded. Over the course of their meetings, some of which lasted several hours, the man who, alongside Mao, governed the largest nation in the world, never gave his American counterpart the impression that he had anything more important to do. Zhou had that talent, so characteristic of great leaders, which consists of giving the person they're talking to the feeling that they command their entire attention. Kissinger would marvel at Zhou's ability to do that.

Over the passing decades, many have been surprised by Kissinger's demonstrative admiration for the Chinese leader. 'I cherish deep feelings for Zhou Enlai,' he would even declare.[8] Beyond the intellectual and personal esteem he had for Zhou Enlai, Kissinger saw the Chinese premier as a soulmate. He knew that, just like him and Nixon, Zhou always had to be on his guard when dealing with a 'boss' who had a somewhat more complex personality. As different as they were in so many ways, Nixon and Mao had a shared tendency towards paranoia, a heightened feeling of insecurity and fits of anger that made them unpredictable.

In the course of his first trip to China from 9 to 11 July 1971, Kissinger was invited to visit the Forbidden City, which was (exceptionally) closed to the public for the occasion. He also had ample opportunity, when not engaged in great conceptual debates with Zhou, to indulge his taste for Chinese cuisine. The banquets were so rich in both quantity and variety of dishes, each more delicious than the last, that Kissinger whispered to one of his colleagues: 'A guest of the state must have starved to death 3,000 years ago and the Chinese are determined that it will not happen again.'[9] A few weeks later, when his secret trip was revealed to the general public, *TIME* magazine noted that: 'When he returned from Peking, an alert observer might have noticed that the man who was supposedly suffering from a stomach ailment had put on five pounds.'[10]

From a diplomatic perspective, Kissinger's first trip to China was a triumph for him. In the forty-page report he wrote up for Nixon upon his return to the United States, he stated: 'We have laid the groundwork for you and Mao to turn a page in history.'[11]

A few days later, on 15 July 1971, Nixon gave a short televised address in which he announced the fledgling rapprochement with the People's Republic of China.

The world was stunned. The president had succeeded in surprising not only the media and his Democratic opponents, but also the Soviets and the North Vietnamese. The North Vietnamese realised that they could no longer count on their powerful Chinese ally to weaken the American troops. As for the USSR, the United States had manoeuvred them into a triangular relationship with China. But Kissinger and Nixon knew full well that such a three-way relationship would only create tensions between the two Communist powers, so pushing the Soviets towards a policy of Détente that the White House so ardently desired.

The rapprochement with China was more than a 'diplomatic coup'. It was also testament to a structural change in American foreign policy.

Until then, the United States tended to view their diplomacy in moral terms. Since the start of the Cold War, they had made themselves the heralds of the camp of good versus the camp of evil, which, in their eyes, was embodied by the non-democratic Communist regimes. Under the influence of Kissinger, this binary logic was replaced by a logic of the balance of powers that took into account factors other than purely moral ones.

In this new diplomatic game, America now had to be prepared to ally with powers whose vision was quite different from its own. This vision of foreign policy, which none of the great adherents of nineteenth-century European *Realpolitik* would have disavowed, carried the seeds of future major successes for America. But this new way would sometimes be hard to digest for an American leadership and public opinion used to draping themselves in comfortable bien-pensant morality.

As much as Kissinger's first trip to Beijing helped to build his legend, it was also the start of a very personal love affair with China. The close ties he developed with Zhou Enlai led to a passion for this country, of which he became an erudite and attentive observer. Over the following five decades, he travelled there close to a hundred times in an attempt to understand this rich and complex civilisation better.

Having grown used to the courtesy, the extraordinary intelligence and the 'elegant professionalism' of Zhou Enlai, as well as Mao's 'philosophical disquisitions and indirect allusions', it took Henry a certain time to adapt to the 'acerbic, no-nonsense style' and 'sarcastic interjections' of their successor, Deng Xiaoping – the man of 'Reform and Opening-up'.[12] Yet both with Deng and the Chinese leaders who followed, Henry eventually managed to nurture very strong relations.

Viewed today in China as a *lao peng you*, or 'old friend', from the West, capable of comprehending Chinese culture and society, the former master of American diplomacy tried, as best he could, to contain the hostility, even malevolence, which has reappeared between Beijing and Washington. Given the defiant attitude towards China omnipresent in the American political sphere, Kissinger feared that the diplomatic manoeuvring between the world's two superpowers was becoming a zero-sum game. He called for the sort of openness and mutual respect that had guided his meetings with Zhou Enlai, and for which he always felt immense nostalgia.

Conclusion

Henry Kissinger was like a rock crystal: he had many facets. A great man, he was vain; seductive, but a manipulator; a strategist and tactician combined; successful, yet riddled with anxiety. To describe his life, we might borrow François Mitterrand's description of his own politics, as he once told it to the writer Jean d'Ormesson: 'neither white nor black, but by necessity grey, with white and black threads'. But whatever Kissinger's ambiguities, his faults and transgressions, it remains an awful thing that Europe lost this man – born in the heart of our continent – to another world power whose interests he devoted his life to defending. In this sense, Henry Kissinger is a European tragedy.

It is a tragedy that Europe must learn from. For it would be an error not to do so, at a time when the European Union is plagued by nationalisms and menaced by powers seeking to weaken or even destroy it. Kissinger's life and work contain many lessons that could allow us to build a strong Europe, capable on its own of preserving our sovereignty and defending the interests of our fellow citizens. Kissinger is a source of hope for all those Europeans who are not resigned to slouching off the stage of history.

Above all, it is by taking inspiration from his actions that we might develop and implement a European *Realpolitik*.

For far too long, the European Union has lost its way in a diplomacy shot through with morals and idealism, but which serves only to isolate and diminish us. Out on the great geopolitical chessboard, we Europeans are no longer writing history. When

Henry Kissinger

it comes to the crises unfolding at our door, those that directly affect our stability, we are not even invited to the negotiating table. Be it in Syria, Yemen or Ukraine, it is our rivals and adversaries who are deciding Europe's future through their decisions. Not so long ago, in the very heart of our continent, in former Yugoslavia, our leaders proved incapable of preventing unforgiveable horror occurring yet again. Disdained by other world powers, the European Union is now losing the respect of its own citizens, little by little.

Worse, we are lying to ourselves. With every outraged declaration by European diplomats condemning the human rights violations and crimes committed by other leaders against their own people, our own leaders boast of having fulfilled their moral contract. But the truth is that our foreign policy has become amoral through its own tragic impotence. Isn't it time to recognise that too few lives have been saved, too few political prisoners released and too few autocrats toppled purely through the magic of our well-intentioned diplomacy?

Our leaders developed a diplomacy suited to the utopian 'end of history' announced by Francis Fukuyama at the end of the Cold War. But in our world of empires and geopolitical competition, such a diplomacy is dangerous, even suicidal for Europe. It is by developing a diplomacy founded in realism – as Kissinger did so brilliantly – that the European Union could be the architect of a global equilibrium that preserves its interests and prevents our continent sinking into chaos. In doing so, Europe would be accomplishing nothing more than continuing the heritage of its greatest diplomats, Metternich, Castlereagh and Talleyrand, in whose footsteps Kissinger trod.

Those who say that the European Union lacks the tools to develop a Kissingerian-style *Realpolitik* forget the strength that the EU's economic power and political stability give it. Its status as the world's leading trading bloc and leading donor of public aid for development are also precious assets in the fashioning of a European *Realpolitik*. It is of course essential that

Conclusion

this be accompanied by the creation of a proper European military arm, without which European diplomacy will continue to lack credibility. But we should not forget that it wasn't where American military power was strongest that Kissinger had his greatest diplomatic successes.

Henry Kissinger's life also demonstrates qualities so cruelly lacking in those currently leading the European Union. As the leaders of EU institutions try to exist in the shadow of those leading its member states – who often carry little weight outside their own national borders – we are in dire need of a European Kissinger.

Henry Kissinger embodied, more than anyone, the figure of the intellectual man of action. When he entered the White House at the age of forty-five, he carried an intellectual heft and a richness of experience built up over several decades of hard work and exposure to a range of situations. This baggage was an important resource in the exercise of his duties and allowed him to develop foreign policy with an eye to the long term.

Yet as intellectual as he was, Kissinger was not disconnected from his time. He was not one of those thinkers who conceived some abstract vision of morality-based foreign policy from the comfort of their ivory tower, free from the weight of diplomatic responsibility. And he certainly was not someone who had accepted being the passive subject of history. He was a man of action who, through his creative and audacious leadership, had the nous to become the architect of a global balance of powers of which the United States remains the referee.

In the era of social media, information at one's fingertips and emotional dials constantly turned to the max, Europe needs, more than ever, to place intellectual men and women of action in its leadership positions, people capable of recalibrating European diplomacy with a long-term perspective, of progressing step by weighed and calculated step, along the lines laid down by Kissinger.

Henry Kissinger

To all those who protest that the position of Europe's top diplomat – formally, the High Representative of the Union for Foreign Affairs and Security Policy – is not a powerful one, Kissinger would argue that it wasn't powerful *yet* because successive holders of that office had not made it so. If Kissinger, as national security advisor, was able to become the master of US diplomacy, it was down to his genius in driving policy and wrangling bureaucracy.

There are currently many leadership positions in the European Union still crying out to be shaped and expanded by those occupying them both now and in the future. But to do this, European leaders must be brave enough to place Europe's interests above their own careers. They must not hesitate to make member states face up to their responsibilities, as much as the member states try to prevent the emergence of a European diplomacy, selfishly focused on their own national issues. This also supposes creating, as Kissinger did, a direct link with European public opinion. All this requires the sort of courage and skill that is too often sorely lacking in the corridors of Brussels.

But there is another essential point on which we have much to learn from Henry Kissinger. In *The Book of Disquiet*, the Portuguese poet Fernando Pessoa, one of the greatest European writers, asks: 'What would happen to the strategist if, with each move he made, he thought of the darkness he cast on a thousand homes and the pain he caused in three thousand hearts?'[1] We might answer that he would become one of our current European leaders, incapable of acting in the face of danger and paralysed by the ever more pressing threats that darken the sky of the European Union. Kissinger, however, courageously stood by certain unpopular decisions and actions when he was convinced they would serve America's interests. He did this knowing full well he would reap the hatred and criticisms of a narrow-minded intelligentsia. There again, his strength of

Conclusion

character must be a model for those presiding over the destiny of the European project.

With Europe facing the return of violence and danger to the continent, it must install a new generation of statesmen and stateswomen at its head. To reach this goal and sketch the blueprint for a new European diplomacy, one which will enable us to write history once more, the figure and the actions of Henry Kissinger are a guide. And if Europe is indeed reborn through taking inspiration from one of its most illustrious children, one who had to flee the continent when it retreated into a maelstrom of its own hatreds and nationalisms, then Henry Kissinger will finally cease to be a European tragedy.

Epilogue

4 March 2022. Nine days since Russia invaded Ukraine. Thousands of miles away from this war, which has plunged Europe back into its darkest days, the icy cold and the heavy snowdrifts beside the road remind me that Connecticut is still very much in winter's grip. It's been over an hour since I left the campus of Yale where I'm due to give a lecture this evening. The countryside seems to get wilder as we drive. Amid the thick, dark forest I spy a myriad of ponds and little lakes. Finally, at the end of a long road near the village of Kent, I finally reach my destination: Henry Kissinger's estate.

It was in 1983 that Henry and Nancy acquired this former farm barely two hours north of New York City. The estate has expanded over the years and now covers more than 250 acres. Henry made this place his bolthole; a peaceful spot in which to write and rest, far from the tumult of New York life. Upon arrival, I am greeted by a butler, as jovial as he is courteous. He leads me into a living room where, flanking a majestic mantelpiece, are numerous objets d'art and paintings recalling Henry's many travels, notably in China. Along the walls stand beautiful bookshelves filled with hundreds of volumes that I like to fancy have nourished both the thoughts and actions of my host.

Suddenly, 'Doctor Kissinger' (as all the household staff call him) enters with Nancy. He walks unsteadily, hunched over, but I am immediately struck by the contrast between this frail body that bears the weight of so many years and the intensity of Henry's gaze. There is a vivacity in his eyes, occasionally tinged with mischief, which, throughout the three hours that follow, will later remind me that this was a man in full possession of his intellectual faculties to the last. His wife, endowed with a natural elegance and refinement, greets me warmly.

As we take our seats in a small adjoining salon bathed in light, Henry, in a barely audible yet firm voice, tells me: 'Jérémie, I ask only one thing: that everything we discuss today, you do not make public while I am alive. Whatever we say to each other, the ideas we share, you can write about them after my death.' As he says these words, I remember anecdotes of journalists complaining that, before each interview, Kissinger would arrive with a bevy of lawyers who would make them sign long agreements in which they undertook not to broach certain sensitive subjects.

I give Henry my word.

At this juncture, I should tell you, dear reader, that I did not make a recording of our meeting, but instead took rough notes, which I wrote up in detail late that night. As such, Henry's words, while faithful in both intent and content, are not necessarily verbatim.

'What is your analysis of the situation in Ukraine?' he asked immediately. I understood at once that since 24 February this man had not stopped attempting to adjust his mental framework to include these ongoing events. He may have been nearing his ninety-ninth birthday, but this individual who had stamped his mark on the history of diplomacy was still driven by an extraordinary intellectual curiosity and the conviction that he still had a role to play through the analyses and advice he furnished to the great and good of this world. 'I have met Putin many times,' he told me. 'In undertaking this assault on Ukraine, he has perhaps committed his greatest error, but I do not believe that he has become an irrational being.' Then he added: 'Anyway, it will be necessary to rebuild a balance of powers in Europe that will not create a situation of permanent insecurity either for Ukraine or for Russia.' Suddenly the telephone rang. Henry excused himself.

Nancy handed me a copy of the controversial column by her

Epilogue

husband that appeared in the *Washington Post* on 5 March 2014, just after Russia's annexation of Crimea and a few weeks before the war in the Donbas broke out. 'Have you read it?' she asked. I nodded. In this piece entitled 'How the Ukraine crisis ends', Henry tried to chart a path that would preserve the values and security interests of both parties. Although he pointed out that Russia should give up trying 'to force Ukraine into a satellite status', he also emphasised that, because of its history, 'Ukraine can never be just a foreign country' in Moscow's eyes.[1] As harsh as he was on the Ukrainian leadership, who he judged lacking in historical perspective and the art of compromise necessary to bring together a country divided by a majority turned towards the West and a Russian-speaking minority, he was no more sparing about the European Union's absence of a strategic vision. He viewed the way the Europeans had conducted negotiations on the Association Agreement between Ukraine and the European Union as a direct cause of the crisis. In this context, he called for Ukraine to become a 'bridge' between East and West. He suggested it take inspiration from Finland, a fiercely independent nation, which cooperates closely with the West in most areas but which – it was not then a member of NATO – 'carefully avoids institutional hostility toward Russia'.[2]

'Please excuse me,' said Henry as he sat back down with us, 'but not a day goes by that I don't receive a call from a head of state or senior official asking my advice.' Then, seeing the copy of his column in front of me: 'I regret not a single word of that piece. A lot of people are now commenting on this war without seeking to understand the historic roots of this conflict and the ties that bind Ukraine to Russia.' He paused, then added: 'Zbigniew Brzeziński agreed with me, you know? Now, you would never accuse him of being "accommodating" as regards Putin, but didn't he too write that Ukraine had no place in NATO?' There was a certain irony in Kissinger using his former rival (both politically and academically) as intellectual backup for his analysis. Nevertheless he was right: on 3 March

2014, Jimmy Carter's national security advisor had also written a column in the *Washington Post* in which he condemned in the strongest possible terms 'the Russian aggression against Ukraine', comparing Putin's way of acting to that of 'a Mafia gangster'. But he also pointed out that 'the West should reassure Russia that it is not seeking to draw Ukraine into NATO or to turn it against Russia'.[3]

Eight years on, though, Kissinger was aware that circumstances had changed. With the Kremlin having sent its troops to capture Kyiv, yet before the war crimes committed by Russian soldiers in Bucha and elsewhere had come to light, Henry knew that many people would use his past writings to caricature his thoughts and reduce him to an amoral figure, lenient with powerful autocrats and blind to the fate of weaker nations. From the start of his career, he had been the object of far too much hatred, jealousy and attacks to ignore it. 'The Russian offensive has changed everything,' he admitted. 'What I once advised, the way I analysed the situation, none of that applies anymore. Now I have to come up with a new frame of reference.' On that day in March, I sat before a man feeling his way, thinking out loud, asking me question after question and tirelessly seeking a suitable strategic vision that might meet both the political and military developments on the ground as well as the way that public opinion would be affected in the longer term. But there was not a single moment during our discussion, or over the months that followed, when he gave in to Manichaeism or an analysis of the facts motivated by pure morality. When, a year later, he would explain his change in position about Ukraine joining NATO, he would justify it by the fact that since this country was now both the best armed in Europe and the one whose leaders were 'the least experienced strategy wise', the best way to avoid it becoming a source of continual instability at the edge of Europe would be to bring it into the North Atlantic alliance so that the West could exercise a certain control over its military decisions. Against the tide of a 'diplomacy of good

Epilogue

intentions' or positions guided solely by the desire to please the Ukrainian leadership and public opinion, Kissinger would adopt the stance he judged to be most suited to ensuring the long-term security of Europe and Russia.

We had been talking for nearly an hour when Nancy stood up. 'Aren't you staying with us?' exclaimed Henry with faux surprise. 'Come on now,' she replied gently, 'I told you I had a lunch date in Kent. And anyway, you can continue chatting just the two of you,' she added, shooting me a smile.

After bidding me goodbye, Nancy gave her husband a discreet yet tender kiss. 'Later, sweetie,' she said as she left the room.

'I believe it's time to sit down to lunch,' Henry announced. One of his bodyguards, a former member of the Dutch special forces, helped him walk to the dining room. On the table, beside a bottle of Bordeaux and one of Pouilly-Fumé, was a copy of the first edition of this book in my original French. As Henry flipped through the pages, I noticed that they were filled with careful notes. 'The reason I wanted to invite you here today, Jérémie, is that this book of yours is the most thoughtful that has ever been written about me.' Staring hard at me, he added: 'I believe you have truly understood me.' Filled with pride, I was momentarily struck dumb. Then a little voice inside reminded me that I was sitting opposite one of the great masters of diplomacy; I had spent three years researching the skill with which he commenced each negotiation, drawing out and winning over the person he was conversing with, never hesitating to resort to flattery. It was evident that this remained an effective technique, particularly with the young Frenchman sat in front of him.

Our conversation shifted to the subject of certain figures who had left their mark on him.

'In your book, you were right to highlight the complexity of my relationship with Nixon. For it was not without tensions. But the more time passes, the more I am convinced that Richard

Henry Kissinger

Nixon was a great president. On the international stage, he was a visionary. The rapprochement with China was his idea. I was merely the facilitator. Détente, he believed in it from the start. Plus, which other of our presidents devoted so much time to foreign affairs and arrived in the White House with such a clear vision of the way he wanted to implement it and the aims he wished to achieve? None, save perhaps George Herbert Bush.' Henry broke off. He seemed pensive. 'Nixon was very unhappy but very brave,' he went on. 'It pained him to be scorned by the liberal elite and the intelligentsia. They never appreciated his true worth. Despite that, he doggedly pursued certain policies, even if he knew how unpopular they were, because he was convinced that they were in the interest of the United States. Watergate aside, I will always hold Nixon in very high regard.

'You know what?' he added. 'Those same liberal elites who always looked down on Nixon are the same who closed the doors of Columbia University to me when I left office.' In 1977, the famous New York university offered a chair in political science to the man who had been in charge of American diplomacy for the past eight years. But a raucous campaign against his appointment, orchestrated by student groups, other Columbia teaching staff and many in the media, resulted in Kissinger giving up on his ambition to return to academia. As I looked at him, I realised that this wound had never fully healed. Despite the honours and the successes he had known in his life, he remained this refugee driven by an insatiable desire for recognition. I also understood that, despite the passing years, he had not become entirely impervious to the fiercest attacks.

Perhaps feeling he had suddenly opened up too much, he switched to talking about Raymond Aron. 'He was extremely generous to me. When we met in the late fifties, I was still only a young academic. He already had a reputation stretching far beyond France's borders. Yet he treated me as an equal. It was only later that our paths parted and that tensions appeared. But despite our disagreements, we always respected each other

Epilogue

and I never stopped admiring his intellectual honesty.' A pause. Then, smiling: 'I think your intuition is correct. Perhaps he too would have wanted to be the "Prince's advisor" to one of your presidents.'

I told Henry that I was working on a new book, about Georges Pompidou. It is my belief that Charles de Gaulle's successor was the most underestimated and least well known of the Fifth Republic. In his memoirs, Kissinger paints a wonderful portrait of this man whose thoughts and actions carry so many lessons for the Europe of today. 'Georges Pompidou was indeed a fascinating figure,' Henry recalled. 'He was a refined man of exceptional intelligence, immensely cultured but who also had very strong convictions. He managed to succeed de Gaulle by stamping his own mark, which was an extraordinary thing in itself. His relations with Nixon were not always smooth but they had deep respect for each other. Our decision to end the convertibility of the dollar into gold might have led to a breakdown, but Pompidou had the intelligence to understand our decision and to try and find a way out for Europe and the United States. He was of enormous help to us during the secret negotiations I led in Paris to end the war in Vietnam.'

I brought up an exchange that Nixon had with Pompidou on 13 December 1971. That day, the French head of state, aware of Europe's extreme dependence on the guarantee of American security, had expressed his wish that Europe equip itself with true joint defensive capabilities. In words that resonate strongly in light of the war in Ukraine and the pivot towards Asia that so many American strategists desire, Pompidou took the following stance:

> Western Europe must forge the greatest possible unity not only in the economic sphere, but also in the political one and, if all goes well, probably with regard to defence too, (...) all the more so because I am sure that the United States will gradually wish to no longer be responsible for the

entire defence of Europe. I have already had occasion to tell you that I did not wish your [the United States'] presence to diminish rapidly, but diminish it will, and Europe must therefore stand strong and united against the East.[4]

Henry smiled. 'It is clear that Pompidou was a visionary on this point too,' he observed. 'Pity that his successors in Europe did not draw the necessary conclusions.'

I asked him about his relationship with Lee Kuan Yew, having been fascinated about the friendship that developed between Kissinger and the founding father of Singapore, two men who, in their youth, had been deeply traumatised by the Nazi regime and the Japanese occupation respectively. 'Lee was an extremely modest person,' explained Henry. 'Over more than four decades, we saw each other many times, in the United States, in Singapore and elsewhere in the world. Our discussions were always very "intellectual". We talked about the international situation, particularly the evolving Sino–American relations. We both knew that we shared a deep bond, but we hardly ever touched on personal matters. There was no room for small talk with Lee.' Henry paused a moment. 'Everything changed when his wife died. I think it was in 2010. Kwa Geok Choo was an extraordinary woman, you know. She was strong, smart. Lee depended on her. Her death left a massive hole in his life. And one day, a few months after Kwa's death – I remember it well because I was right here – I got a call from Lee. He just wanted to talk, about anything and everything. From then until his death, we called each other often, just as friends would.'

'Was he the leader who made the greatest impression on you?' Henry thought for a few moments. 'In your book, you also mention my relationship with Zhou Enlai. He and Lee are of course figures who influenced me deeply. But the more I think about it, the more I tell myself that perhaps it was Sadat who I admired the most. Like many people, I underestimated him at first. Yet he was not only a visionary but also incredibly

Epilogue

brave. Without that courage, which cost him his life, nothing we accomplished in the Middle East would have been possible.'

The butler brought in a cheese plate, and as I finally yielded to the temptation to try the Bordeaux, I asked Henry what he thought about the new Moscow–Beijing axis. A month earlier, at the opening ceremony of the Winter Olympics in Beijing, Xi Jinping and Vladimir Putin had published a long joint statement on 'Deepening the China–Russia Comprehensive Strategic Partnership of Coordination for the New Era'. Henry's response was terse. 'It's a rapprochement of circumstance. I believe that it is neither solid nor sustainable. Throughout my career, I have only ever witnessed immense reciprocal mistrust between the leaders of these two countries.'

In this context, how should Europe position itself in relation to China? 'You should not be naive with regard to Beijing,' emphasised Henry. 'China is a competitor – even a dangerous rival – to Europe in many areas, be it economically, technologically or politically. But Europeans must also take care not to fall into the sort of anti-Chinese hysteria that has seized much of the Washington elite. Indeed, as you've probably noticed, the Biden administration does not have such a different approach to Beijing than the Trump administration did. The method is less unilateralist and relies more on the strength of our alliances, but the underlying idea remains the same: China is an enemy whose rise must be slowed at any price. This is an error.'

He cast his eye around the table to see where his Labrador was in order to give her a couple of treats. Then he continued. 'Biden is surrounded by experienced and skilled people. Bill Burns is one. But where is this administration's strategic vision? Europe is right to try and tread its own path in relation to China. But you have a huge weakness: your credibility is stymied by your lack of military power. Yet history teaches us that it has always been hard to influence world affairs without defensive capabilities worthy of the name.'

It was now Henry's turn to shift the focus of our discussion.

Henry Kissinger

'There is another weakness which distinguishes Europe from the United States. In the conclusion of your book, you write that I am a "European tragedy". I understand what you were getting at. But there is something you should be aware of: a middle-class Jewish boy such as I was would never have had the sort of life and career in Europe that I was able to have in the United States.' Which prompted me to ask: 'Doctor Kissinger, I admit that there is a certain conservatism undermining Europe and that social mobility is all too often just an illusion there. But do you think that this American dream you evoke still exists? Do you believe that if a young refugee were to set foot in the United States today, penniless and without a word of English, as was your case in 1938, could they hope to become secretary of state one day?'

'That's a good question,' replied Henry. 'I don't know.'

Coffee was served: mine in a beautiful porcelain cup, Henry's in a large mug printed with a photograph of his beloved Labrador. As I endeavoured to tear my eyes away from this object, which I would never have imagined in such an elegant setting, Henry went on: 'You wrote a chapter about my mother. She was a remarkable woman but, you know, my father was also an exceptional man in his own way. In fact, I noticed that you dedicated this book to your own father.' I told Henry about my father and how much he was, and remains, a model for me. He left us not long before this book was first published in France.

Lunch was coming to an end. Before parting, Henry gave me one final piece of advice: 'Jérémie, you seem driven by the desire to build a stronger European diplomacy. That is a fine and grand ambition but it is a huge task. You have no time to lose.'

After Henry had left, I tried to call an Uber to take me back to New Haven. But in this remote corner of Connecticut, it was a cause already lost. So one of Henry's security detail was kind enough to ask a friend of his to come and get me. After waiting around for close to twenty minutes, during which Henry's bodyguards spoke to me with great affection of the pride they felt

Epilogue

in serving 'Doctor Kissinger' – whose huge capacity for hard work they all highlighted – a large pickup truck bearing a massive 'TRUMP' sticker pulled up. During the next hour and a half, my driver, a former Bronx police officer originally from Puerto Rico, talked to me about his son, also now a member of the NYPD, and recounted his fishing and hunting trips in the surrounding rivers and woods with great enthusiasm. He asked me about the reasons for my visit and the subject of the war in Ukraine came up. 'If it was up to me,' he declared firmly, 'I'd bomb Moscow!' I couldn't suppress an inner smile as I imagined how Henry would respond to such a suggestion.

As the magnificent buildings of Yale campus pulled into view, I recalled Henry's last words to me when we parted: 'Drop by and see me next time you're in the US. I'll be very happy to continue our discussion.' Unfortunately I would never get the chance. Henry Kissinger died on 29 November 2023.

Chronology

27 May 1923. Birth of Heinz Alfred Kissinger into an orthodox Jewish family in Fürth, a few miles from Nuremberg. Eldest son of Louis and Paula Kissinger. His younger brother, Walter, is born in June 1924.

September 1935. Louis Kissinger is fired from his teaching post following the introduction of the Nuremberg Laws, which removed German citizenship from Jews and other 'non-German' minority groups.

August 1938. With antisemitic hatred and violence becoming ever more acute, Paula Kissinger decides that the time has come for her family to flee Germany. Less than three months before Kristallnacht, the Kissingers leave for New York, stopping briefly in London.

September 1938. The Kissingers make their home in a modest apartment in Washington Heights in northwest Manhattan. With a population composed mainly of German Jewish refugees, the neighbourhood is dubbed the 'Fourth Reich' by New Yorkers. Heinz changes his name to Henry.

1941. After passing his high-school diploma at George Washington High School with flying colours, Kissinger somewhat unenthusiastically embarks on accountancy studies at the City College of New York.

Henry Kissinger

March 1943. Henry Kissinger is mobilised into the US Army. For the first time in his life, he finds himself living in an environment that is not entirely composed of German Jews. On 19 June 1943, he becomes a naturalised American at Camp Croft, a military training base in South Carolina.

June 1943. Henry's intellectual qualities are quickly spotted and he is enrolled on the Army Specialized Training Program and sent to Lafayette College in Pennsylvania to study engineering.

Summer 1944. After the Allied invasion of Normandy, additional troops are required to go and fight at the front. Kissinger is posted to Camp Claiborne in Louisiana for further training. Here he makes the acquaintance of Fritz Kraemer, who would become his first mentor and have a decisive influence on his life.

September 1944–July 1947. Kissinger is deployed to Germany, wearing the uniform of the US Army. After the end of the war in Europe, he remains mobilised in the country of his birth where he takes part in the campaign of denazification.

August 1947. Kissinger enters Harvard University to study political science. After submitting an undergraduate dissertation entitled 'The meaning of history: reflections on Spengler, Toynbee and Kant', he gets his master's degree in 1951, followed by his doctorate in 1954. His thesis, 'A world restored: Metternich, Castlereagh and the problems of peace, 1812–1822', is published in 1957. At Harvard, Kissinger follows the lectures of William Yandell Elliott, who has a strong influence on him.

6 February 1949. Kissinger marries his childhood sweetheart, Ann Fleischer, whom he met in Washington Heights. They later have a daughter, Elizabeth, and a son, David. Ann and Henry divorce in 1964.

Chronology

1955–56. Kissinger joins the Council on Foreign Relations in New York, where he runs a working group on nuclear deterrence. Kissinger meets Nelson Rockefeller.

1957. Kissinger publishes *Nuclear Weapons and Foreign Policy*, in which he criticises the strategy of 'massive retaliation' espoused by President Dwight Eisenhower in the context of the Cold War. Instead he calls for the implementation of a policy of 'flexible response' towards the Soviet bloc. The book garners him considerable renown in political and academic circles.

1959. Henry Kissinger is made associate professor at Harvard University. He teaches there until 1968.

1961. Kissinger publishes *Necessity for Choice: Prospects of American Foreign Policy* as he seeks to build his influence in the political sphere and burnish his image as a future 'Prince's advisor'.

1956–68. Kissinger starts working for Nelson Rockefeller, becoming one of his closest collaborators. He advises Rockefeller on issues of foreign policy and plays an active part in the New York governor's three presidential campaigns of 1960, 1964 and 1968.

20 January 1969. Richard Nixon, the newly elected president of the United States, appoints Kissinger as his national security advisor. Kissinger's decision to join the Nixon administration is seen as a betrayal by Rockefeller's people.

1969–70. During the war in Vietnam, Kissinger convinces Nixon to undertake a secret bombing campaign in Cambodia and Laos to weaken the Viet Cong's rear. Kissinger was heavily criticised for these air raids, which caused many civilian casualties.

Henry Kissinger

July and October 1971. Kissinger makes two trips to Beijing to meet Zhou Enlai and work on a rapprochement between the People's Republic of China and the United States. These diplomatic manoeuvres result in President Nixon's historic visit to China from 21 to 28 February 1972.

1972. Kissinger negotiates the SALT I (Strategic Arms Limitations Talks) agreement with the Soviet leadership. Its aim is to limit the nuclear arsenals of the two superpowers and is part of the policy of Détente, which Kissinger, in conjunction with Nixon, wishes to pursue with the USSR. He receives a lot of criticism of this policy of Détente, both within the United States and among his European allies, who see the establishment of this new balance of powers as threatening their own security.

27 January 1973. The United States and North Vietnam sign the Paris Peace Accords, following which Kissinger and Lê Đức Thọ jointly receive the Nobel Peace Prize in recognition of their efforts to end the war in Vietnam. Lê Đức Thọ declines this Nobel Prize because, in his view, 'peace has not yet really been established'. Eighteen months later, following the invasion of South Vietnam by the Communist troops of North Vietnam, Kissinger tries to return the prize. His gesture is declined.

11 September 1973. A coup d'état against Chilean president Salvador Allende is orchestrated by General Augusto Pinochet, commander-in-chief of the armed forces, with the support of the United States. Allende dies that day and Pinochet takes power, ushering in a long period of military dictatorship.

22 September 1973. Kissinger takes the oath of office as secretary of state of the United States. He remains national security advisor in parallel until 3 November 1975, the only secretary of state to have held both posts simultaneously.

Chronology

6 October 1973. Egypt and Syria launch a joint attack against Israel, so starting the Yom Kippur War. With Nixon mired in the Watergate scandal, it is Kissinger who supervises the American response to this crisis. While making Israel's survival his absolute priority, he tries to create the conditions for a lasting peace in the Middle East. The conflict marks the starting point for the strong relationship that would form between Kissinger and the Egyptian president, Anwar Sadat.

30 March 1974. Kissinger marries his second wife, Nancy Maginnes, whom he had met when they were both campaigning for Nelson Rockefeller. This marriage to a non-Jewish woman is frowned upon by some of the Orthodox Jewish community.

9 August 1974. Threatened with impeachment because of the Watergate scandal, Richard Nixon resigns the presidency of the United States. He is succeeded by his vice president, Gerald Ford, who decides to keep Kissinger in post. However, on 3 November 1975, Ford removes Kissinger's other role of national security advisor and gives it to Lieutenant General Brent Scowcroft.

1975. For the third year running, Henry Kissinger tops Gallup's list of men whom Americans admire the most.

20 January 1977. Following Jimmy Carter's election as president of the United States, Kissinger leaves office. He decides to return to academia and is offered a chair at New York's Columbia University, but the proposal is met with a wave of protests by students and staff. He accepts a professorship at Washington's Georgetown University instead.

1979. Henry Kissinger publishes the first volume of his memoirs, *White House Years*.

1982. Kissinger founds his own consultancy, Kissinger Associates, aimed at advising leaders and world figures on geopolitical issues and international investment opportunities. Many copycat consultancies would attempt to emulate Kissinger Associates, often without success.

November 2002. President George W. Bush appoints Kissinger to chair the National Commission on Terrorist Attacks Upon the United States (also known as the 9-11 Commission). But the former secretary of state resigns on 13 December to avoid having to reveal the client list of Kissinger Associates – requested to ensure no conflict of interest.

2014. After the success of *On China* three years previously, comes *World Order*, in which Kissinger explores the possibility of building a new international order in an age of huge technological upheaval where the dominant powers are driven by very different historical, cultural and ideological perspectives.

2021. Kissinger's book on artificial intelligence, co-written with Eric Schmidt and Daniel Huttenlocher, is published. This is the fruit of Kissinger's work since 2018 to attempt, as a historian and expert in international relations, to understand the consequences of artificial intelligence, which he saw as the greatest challenge of our time.

2022. Kissinger publishes his final book, *Leadership: Six Studies in World Strategy*, in which he analyses the figures of Konrad Adenauer, Charles de Gaulle, Margaret Thatcher, Lee Kuan Yew, Anwar Sadat and Richard Nixon.

29 November 2023. Henry Kissinger dies at his estate in Kent, Connecticut, at the age of 100. Right to the end of his life, he remained a highly influential commentator and analyst of international relations whose advice was sought by leaders across the world.

Selective bibliography

Many biographies of Henry Kissinger have been published, most of them in the United States. Walter Isaacson's, which appeared in 1992, remains one of the fullest and finest in my view, because of its depth and its style. Henry Kissinger was also the author of many standout books, for which he had no equal (or almost none) in the field of international relations. Of the numerous sources that fed my reflections and my writing, I have chosen to mention below some of the works that I particularly appreciated.

Works by Henry Kissinger

A World Restored: Metternich, Castlereagh and the Problems of Peace, 1812–1822, Boston, Houghton Mifflin, 1957
White House Years, Boston, Little, Brown and Company, 1979
Years of Upheaval, Boston, Little, Brown and Company, 1982
Diplomacy, New York, Simon & Schuster, 1994
Years of Renewal, Boston, Little, Brown and Company, 1999
Does America Need a Foreign Policy? Toward a Diplomacy for the 21st Century, New York, Simon & Schuster, 2001
Ending the Vietnam War: A History of America's Involvement in and Extrication from the Vietnam War, New York, Simon & Schuster, 2003
Crisis: The Anatomy of Two Major Foreign Policy Crises, New York, Simon & Schuster, 2004
On China, New York, Penguin Press, 2011
World Order, New York, Penguin Press, 2014
The Age of AI: And Our Human Future (co-authored with Eric

Schmidt and Daniel Huttenlocher), Boston, Little, Brown and Company, 2021

Leadership: Six Studies in World Strategy, New York, Penguin Press, 2022

Works on Henry Kissinger

David Landau, *Kissinger: The Uses of Power*, Boston, Houghton Mifflin, 1972

Danielle Hunebelle, *Dear Henry*, Paris, Gallimard, 1972

Marvin Kalb and Bernard Kalb, *Kissinger*, Boston, Little, Brown and Company, 1974

William Safire, *Before the Fall*, New York, Doubleday, 1975

Richard Valeriani, *Travels with Henry*, Boston, Houghton Mifflin, 1979

Walter Isaacson, *Kissinger: A Biography*, New York, Simon & Schuster, 1992

Robert Dallek, *Nixon and Kissinger: Partners in Power*, New York, HarperCollins, 2007

Charles Zorgbibe, *Kissinger*, Paris, Editions de Fallois, 2015

Niall Ferguson, *Kissinger: 1923–1968: The Idealist*, New York, Penguin Press, 2015

Winston Lord, *Kissinger on Kissinger: Reflections on Diplomacy, Grand Strategy, and Leadership*, New York, All Points Books, 2019

Barry Gewen, *The Inevitability of Tragedy: Henry Kissinger and His World*, New York, W.W. Norton & Company, 2020

Robert B. Zoellick, *America in the World: A History of US Diplomacy and Foreign Policy*, New York, Twelve, 2020

Gérard Araud, *Henry Kissinger: Le diplomate du siècle*, Paris, Tallandier, 2021

Martin Indyk, *Master of the Game: Henry Kissinger and the Art of Middle East Diplomacy*, New York, Knopf, 2021

Acknowledgements

I thank my mother for her precious advice, her attentive proof-reading and for having passed on her love of books to me.

I also thank Katie for her steadfast support and all that she brings me day after day.

Without them, this book would never have come to fruition.

The translator would like to give a respectful nod to Victor Salem who, as shipping officer at the US embassy in Paris, helped with the logistics for the negotiations that led to the Paris Peace Accords of 1973.

Notes

Foreword
1. Henry Kissinger, *Diplomacy*, Simon & Schuster, 1994, p.471.
2. Henry Kissinger, *A World Restored: Metternich, Castlereagh and the Problems of Peace, 1812–1822*, Boston, Houghton Mifflin, 1957, p. 322.
3. Kallol Bhattacherjee, 'Kissinger, Nixon "helped" Pakistan in 1971, documents from U.S. Archive reveal', *The Hindu*, 1 December 2023; Robert Evans, 'Henry Kissinger's role in Bengali massacre', *Guardian*, 4 December 2023.

De Gaulle
1. Yves-Henri Nouailhat, 'Nixon–de Gaulle: un épisode original des relations franco-américaines', *Revue française d'études américaines*, 32, April 1987, pp. 309–18.
2. Declaration by Dwight D. Eisenhower regarding the European Defence Community, 16 April 1954.
3. Henry Kissinger, 'The Illusionist: why we misread de Gaulle', *Harper's Magazine*, March 1965.
4. Ibid.
5. Ibid.
6. Henry Kissinger, 'Strains on the Alliance', *Foreign Affairs*, January 1963.
7. Ibid.
8. Richard Nixon, *Leaders*, London, Sidgwick & Jackson, 1982, p. 44.
9. Public Papers of the President of the United States, Richard Nixon, containing the Public Messages, Speeches and Statements of the President 1969, US Government Printing Office, Washington DC, 1971, no. 88.
10. Ibid.

Notes

11 Richard Nixon, *RN: The Memoirs of Richard Nixon*, New York, Simon & Schuster, 1978, pp. 373–4.
12 Henry Kissinger, *White House Years*, Boston, Little, Brown and Company, 1979, p. 110.
13 Nixon, *Leaders*, op. cit., p. 76.
14 Maurice Ferro, *De Gaulle et l'Amérique, une amitié tumultueuse*, Paris, Plon, 1973, p. 430.
15 Kissinger, *White House Years*, op. cit., pp. 387–8.
16 Ibid., p. 388.
17 Ibid.
18 Kenneth S. Levine, 'Henry Kissinger relates time spent with De Gaulle', *Columbia Daily Spectator*, CXIV (108), 9 April 1990.
19 'Henry Kissinger on Europe's falling out with Washington', *Der Spiegel*, 10 October 2005.
20 Charles de Gaulle, *Le fil de l'épée*, Paris, Perrin, 2015 (1st edn, Plon, 1932), pp. 62–3.

Football

1 See H.R. Haldeman, *The Ends of Power*, New York, Times Books, 1978.
2 See Brian Kilmeade, *The Games Do Count: America's Best and Brightest on the Power of Sports*, New York, HarperCollins, 2005.
3 Henry Kissinger, 'World Cup according to character', *Los Angeles Times*, 29 June 1986.
4 Steve James, 'Henry Kissinger: diplomat, Nobel laureate, soccer fan', *Reuters LIFE!*, 6 April 2009.
5 Alfred Santasiere III, '5 Minutes with Henry Kissinger', *Yankees Magazine*, August 2012.
6 Paul Simpson, 'The Fürth fan', *Blizzard*, 33, 7 June 2019.
7 James, 'Henry Kissinger: diplomat, Nobel laureate, soccer fan', op. cit.
8 Robert Hennemeyer, 'The day Henry Kissinger watched Johan Cruyff play against Brazil' (Letter to the Editor), *Washington Post*, 31 March 2016.

9 Simpson, 'The Fürth fan, op. cit.
10 Dave Hannigan, 'How Henry Kissinger spoke football when playing politics', *Irish Times*, 10 October 2017.
11 Ibid.
12 Ibid.
13 Jack Holmes, 'How Henry Kissinger convinced Pelé to play soccer in the US', *Esquire*, 13 May 2016.
14 Ibid.
15 Memorandum by Henry A. Kissinger for the attention of President Gerald Ford, 28 June 1975, Library of Congress, document no. LOC-HAK-74-5-2-2.
16 Simpson, 'The Fürth fan', op. cit.
17 Alexander Wolff, 'It should be a kick', *Sports Illustrated*, 20 June 1994.
18 Roger Cohen, 'When Kissinger calls, it's World Cup time', *New York Times*, 14 June 2010.
19 Ibid.
20 George Vecsey, 'Kissinger's new mission: bring World Cup to the US', *New York Times*, 30 March 2009.

Glamour

1 'It's Super K!', *Newsweek*, 10 June 1974.
2 Walter Isaacson, *Kissinger: A Biography*, New York, Simon & Schuster, 1992, p. 359.
3 Ibid., p. 356.
4 Hedrick Smith, 'Foreign policy: Kissinger at hub', *New York Times*, 19 January 1971.
5 Sally Quinn, *Washington Post*, 10 October 1969.
6 Barbara Walters, 'Interview with Henry Kissinger', NBC, 3 May 1975.
7 Kandy Stroud, 'I wonder who's kissing now', *Women's Wear Daily*, 8 September 1971.
8 Ibid.
9 Isaacson, *Kissinger: A Biography*, op. cit., p. 365.
10 Ralph Blumenfeld, *Henry Kissinger: The Private and Public Story*, New York, Signet Books, 1974, p. 226.

Notes

11 Isaacson, *Kissinger: A Biography*, op. cit., p. 370.
12 Oriana Fallaci, 'Kissinger rivela', *L'Europeo*, 16 November 1972.
13 Isaacson, *Kissinger: A Biography*, op. cit., p. 364.
14 Ibid.
15 H.R. Haldeman, Memorandum from Haldeman to Alexander Butterfield, 9 February 1971, Haldeman papers, box 196, WHSF, NPP.
16 Joseph Kraft, 'Henry Kissinger, the virtuoso, at 50', *Washington Post*, 27 May 1973.
17 Isaacson, *Kissinger: A Biography*, op. cit., p. 589.

Harvard

1 Richard Norton Smith, *The Harvard Century*, New York, Simon & Schuster, 1986, pp. 168–78.
2 Barbara Campbell, 'Dr. William Y. Elliott, 82, Dies; A Harvard Professor Emeritus', *New York Times*, 11 January 1979.
3 Walter Isaacson, *Kissinger: A Biography*, New York, Simon & Schuster, 1992, p. 63.
4 Henry Kissinger, 'Kissinger tribute to William Elliott', Archives of Harvard University, Pusey Library.
5 Henry Kissinger, 'The meaning of history: reflections on Spengler, Toynbee and Kant', undergraduate thesis, Harvard University, 1950.
6 Henry Kissinger, 'Peace, legitimacy, and the equilibrium: a study of the statesmanship of Castlereagh and Metternich', dissertation, Harvard University, 1954.
7 Henry Kissinger, *Nuclear Weapons and Foreign Policy*, New York, Council on Foreign Relations/Harper & Brothers, 1957.
8 Woody Allen, *Annie Hall*, United Artists, 1977.
9 Henry Kissinger, 'The White Revolutionary: reflections on Bismarck', *Daedalus*, summer 1968.
10 Henry Kissinger, application to the Graduate School of Arts and Sciences, Archives of Harvard University.

Henry Kissinger

Helsinki

1. A. Denis Clift, Memorandum from A. Denis Clift of the National Security Council Staff to the President's Assistant for National Security Affairs (Kissinger), Office of the Historian, United States Department of State, 26 June 1975.
2. 'Kissinger sees perils in Solzhenitsyn's views', *New York Times*, 17 July 1975.
3. Aleksandr Solzhenitsyn, 'The voice of freedom'. Speech given to the AFL-CIO in Washington on 30 June 1975.
4. See Samuel Pisar, *Les armes de la paix*, Paris, Denoël, 1970.
5. Fred Barnes, 'White House moving on Solzhenitsyn', *Washington Star*, 15 July 1975.
6. Philip Shabecoff, 'Ford avoided visit by Solzhenitsyn', *New York Times*, 3 July 1975.
7. Bernard Gwertzman, 'Solzhenitsyn says Ford joins in Eastern Europe's "Betrayal"', *New York Times*, 22 July 1975.
8. Aleksandr Solzhenitsyn, Speech given before the Congress of the United States, 15 July 1975. Reproduced in *Warning to the West*, New York, Farrar Straus and Giroux, 1976, pp. 91–6.
9. Henry Kissinger, 'The moral foundations of foreign policy'. Speech given in Minneapolis, 15 July 1975.
10. Lou Cannon and Don Oberdorfer, 'Reagan praises Helsinki Accords' achievements', *Washington Post*, 28 May 1988.
11. Gerald Ford, 'President Gerald R. Ford's address in Helsinki before the Conference on Security and Cooperation in Europe', Helsinki, 25 July 1975.
12. Leonid Brezhnev, 'Speech by Leonid Brezhnev', Helsinki, 31 July 1975.
13. Walter Isaacson, *Kissinger: A Biography*, New York, Simon & Schuster, 1992, p. 663.
14. Thomas F. DeFrank, *Write It When I'm Gone: Remarkable Off-the-record Conversations with Gerald R. Ford*, New York, G. P. Putnam's Sons, 2007, pp. 89–90.

Notes

Humour

1. Edward Teller, 'A new look at war-making', *New York Times*, 7 July 1957.
2. Walter Isaacson, *Kissinger: A Biography*, New York, Simon & Schuster, 1992, p. 88.
3. David Reynolds, *Six Meetings That Shaped the Twentieth Century*, New York, Basic Books, 2007, p. 230.
4. William Safire, *Before the Fall*, New York, Doubleday, 1975, p. 157.
5. Warren Bass, *Support Any Friend: Kennedy's Middle East and the Making of the US–Israel Alliance*, Oxford, Oxford University Press, 2004, p. 154.
6. Isaacson, *Kissinger: A Biography*, op. cit., p. 193.
7. Safire, *Before the Fall*, op. cit., p. 391.
8. Kandy Stroud, 'I wonder who's kissing now', *Women's Wear Daily*, 8 September 1971.
9. Ibid.
10. Henry Kissinger, *A World Restored: Metternich, Castlereagh and the Problems of Peace, 1812–1822*, Boston, Houghton Mifflin, 1957, p. 8.
11. Edward R. F. Sheehan, *The Arabs, Israelis, and Kissinger: A Secret History of American Diplomacy in the Middle East*, New York, Readers Digest Press, 1976, p. 95.
12. Isaacson, *Kissinger: A Biography*, op. cit., p. 193.

Indefensible?

1. Christopher Hitchens, *The Trial of Henry Kissinger*, London, Verso, 2001.
2. Jon Nordheimer, 'Reagan, in direct attack, assails Ford on defense', *New York Times*, 5 March 1976.
3. Richard L. Strout, 'Kissinger–Reagan huddle results in apparent foreign policy "détente"', *Christian Science Monitor*, 16 July 1980.
4. Christopher Hitchens, 'The case against Henry Kissinger', *Harper's Magazine*, February 2001.

5   Taylor Owen and Ben Kiernan, 'Bombs over Cambodia', *Walrus*, October 2006.
6   See Ben Kiernan, *Pol Pot Regime*, New Haven, Yale University Press, 1996.
7   Gary J. Bass, 'Nixon and Kissinger's forgotten shame', *New York Times*, 29 September 2013.
8   Ellen Barry, 'To U.S. in '70s, a dissenting diplomat. To Bangladesh, "a true friend"', *New York Times*, 27 June 2016.
9   Michael Richardson, 'Ford and Kissinger had bigger problems/"We will understand and will not press you": how U.S. averted gaze when Indonesia took East Timor', *International Herald Tribune*, 20 May 2002.
10 Walter Isaacson, *Kissinger: A Biography*, New York, Simon & Schuster, 1992, pp. 680-1.
11 Uki Goni, 'Kissinger hindered US effort to end mass killings in Argentina, according to files', *Guardian*, 9 August 2016.
12 Seymour M. Hersh, 'Kissinger called Chile strategist', *New York Times*, 15 September 1974.
13 Testimony before the Church Committee, 13 July 1975 (declassified in 1994).
14 Larry Rohter, 'Word for word/Kissinger on Pinochet; the human rights crowd gives realpolitik the jitters', *New York Times*, 28 December 2003.
15 Alvin Shuster, 'Kissinger's role in Cyprus crisis criticized', *New York Times*, 19 August 1974.
16 Hitchens, *The Trial of Henry Kissinger*, op. cit.
17 See Barry Gewen, *The Inevitability of Tragedy: Henry Kissinger and His World*, New York, W.W. Norton & Company, 2020.
18 Seymour M. Hersh, *The Price of Power: Kissinger in the Nixon White House*, New York, Simon & Schuster, 1983, pp. 46-8.
19 See David Landau, *Kissinger: The Uses of Power*, Boston, Houghton Mifflin, 1972, pp. 157-60.
20 Theo Sommer, 'Handeln, als wäre Amerika unsterblich', *Die Zeit*, 2 July 1976, cited in William Shawcross, *Sideshow: Kissinger, Nixon and the Destruction of Cambodia*, New York, Simon & Schuster, 1979, p. 393.

21 Ibid.
22 Isaacson, *Kissinger: A Biography*, op. cit., p. 274.
23 Testimony of Henry Kissinger before the House Foreign Affairs Committee, 18 April 1975.
24 Philip Short, *Pol Pot: The History of a Nightmare*, London, John Murray, 2005.
25 Robert D. Kaplan, 'In Defense of Henry Kissinger. He was the 20th century's greatest 19th-century statesman', *Atlantic*, May 2013.
26 Charles Zorgbibe, *Kissinger*, Paris, Éditions de Fallois, 2015, p. 395.
27 Regarding the 'grey area' concept, see Henry Kissinger, 'Military policy and defense of the "grey areas"', *Foreign Affairs*, April 1955.
28 See Gary J. Bass, *The Blood Telegram: Nixon, Kissinger, and a Forgotten Genocide*, New York, Knopf, 2013.
29 Henry Kissinger, *Years of Renewal*, Boston, Little, Brown and Company, 1999.

Jewishness

1 Elie Wiesel, *Night* (trans. Marion Wiesel), London, Penguin, 2008.
2 William Safire, *Before the Fall*, New York, Doubleday, 1975, p. 564.
3 George Lardner Jr and Michael Dobbs, 'New tapes reveal depth of Nixon's anti-Semitism', Washington Post, 6 October 1999.
4 Henry Kissinger, *Years of Upheaval*, Boston, Little, Brown and Company, 1982, p. 202.
5 Lardner and Dobbs, 'New tapes reveal depth of Nixon's anti-Semitism', op. cit.
6 Seymour M. Hersh, 'Kissinger and Nixon in the White House', *Atlantic*, May 1982.
7 Kissinger, *Years of Upheaval*, op. cit., pp. 202–3.
8 Isi Leibler, 'Kissinger, court Jews and anti-Semites', *Jerusalem Post*, 16 December 2010.

9 Walter Isaacson, *Kissinger: A Biography*, op. cit., pp. 561–2.
10 Clyde Haberman, 'Decades later, Kissinger's words stir fresh outrage among Jews', *New York Times*, 16 December 2010.
11 Moshe Phillips, 'US Jews shouldn't honor Kissinger', *Jerusalem Post*, 6 July 2019.
12 Gil Troy, 'Happy birthday, Mr. Kissinger', *Tablet Magazine*, 23 May 2013.
13 See Gil Troy, *Moynihan's Moment: America's Fight Against Zionism as Racism*, Oxford, Oxford University Press, 2012.
14 Henry Kissinger, Speech given on the occasion of the presentation of the Stephen Wise Award to Golda Meir, 13 November 1977.
15 Bernard Gwertzman, 'Now, Kissinger woos his critics', *New York Times*, 19 January 1977.
16 Michael Kramer, 'American Jews and Israel: the schism', *New York Magazine*, 18 October 1982.

Lee Kuan Yew

1 Graham Allison, 'The sayings of Lee Kuan Yew, the sage of Singapore', *Los Angeles Times*, 25 March 2015.
2 Henry Kissinger, 'Henry A. Kissinger: the world will miss Lee Kuan Yew', *Washington Post*, 23 March 2015.
3 Graham Allison and Robert D. Blackwill, *Lee Kuan Yew: The Grand Master's Insights on China, the United States, and the World – Foreword by Henry A. Kissinger*, Cambridge, MIT Press, 2013, p. ix.
4 Ibid., p. 137.
5 Kissinger, 'Henry A. Kissinger: the world will Miss Lee Kuan Yew', op. cit.
6 Ibid.
7 Robert D. Blackwill, 'Lee Kuan Yew and Henry Kissinger', *National Interest*, 13 April 2015.
8 Allison and Blackwill, *Lee Kuan Yew: The Grand Master's Insights on China, the United States, and the World*, op. cit., p. vii.

Notes

9 Winston Churchill, Speech in the House of Commons, 11 November 1947.
10 Allison and Blackwill, *Lee Kuan Yew*, op. cit., pp. 25–6.
11 Francis Fukuyama, *The End of History and the Last Man*, New York, Free Press, 1992.
12 World Bank and OECD national accounts data. Source: https://data.worldbank.org/indicator/NY.GDP.PCAP.CD?locations=SG
13 Kissinger, 'Henry A. Kissinger: The World Will Miss Lee Kuan Yew', op. cit.
14 Lee Kuan Yew, *The Singapore Story: Memoirs of Lee Kuan Yew*, Singapore, Times Editions, Singapore Press Holdings, 1998, p. 8.

Mentor

1 Barnard Law Collier, 'The road to Peking, or, how does this Kissinger do it?', *New York Times*, 14 November 1971.
2 Ibid.
3 Henry A. Kissinger speaking at the funeral service for Fritz Kraemer, Arlington, Fort Myer Chapel, 8 October 2003.
4 Walter Isaacson, *Kissinger: A Biography*, New York, Simon & Schuster, 1992, p. 44.
5 Collier, 'The road to Peking', op. cit.
6 Henry A. Kissinger speaking at the funeral service for Fritz Kraemer, Arlington, Fort Myer Chapel, 8 October 2003.
7 Isaacson, *Kissinger: A Biography*, op. cit., p. 45.
8 Peter F. Drucker, 'How Fritz Kraemer, "The enemy of publicity", shaped Kissinger's thoughts and actions', *New York Times*, 19 February 1979.
9 Isaacson, *Kissinger: A Biography*, op. cit., p. 671.
10 Henry A. Kissinger speaking at the funeral service for Fritz Kraemer, Arlington, Fort Myer Chapel, 8 October 2003.
11 Michael T. Kaufman, 'Fritz Kraemer, 95, tutor to US generals and Kissinger, dies', *New York Times*, 19 November 2003.
12 Henry A. Kissinger speaking at the funeral service for Fritz Kraemer, Arlington, Fort Myer Chapel, 8 October 2003.

Metternich

1. Walter Isaacson, *Kissinger: A Biography*, New York, Simon & Schuster, 1992, p. 77.
2. Henry Kissinger, *A World Restored: Metternich, Castlereagh and the Problems of Peace, 1812–1822*, Boston, Houghton Mifflin, 1957, pp. 9–12.
3. Isaacson, *Kissinger: A Biography*, op. cit., p. 556.
4. Henry Kissinger, *Diplomacy*, New York, Simon & Schuster, 1994.
5. Isaacson, *Kissinger: A Biography*, op. cit., p. 554.
6. Ibid.
7. Robert D. Kaplan, 'Kissinger, Metternich, and realism', *Atlantic*, June 1999.
8. Kissinger, *A World Restored*, op. cit., p. 19.
9. Ibid, p. 83.

Nixon

1. David Landau, *Kissinger: The Uses of Power*, Boston, Houghton Mifflin, 1972, p. 89.
2. Marvin Kalb and Bernard Kalb, *Kissinger*, Boston, Little, Brown and Company, 1974, p. 15.
3. Landau, *Kissinger: The Uses of Power*, op. cit., p. 88.
4. Walter Isaacson, *Kissinger: A Biography*, New York, Simon & Schuster, 1992, p. 131.
5. Richard Nixon, *RN: The Memoirs of Richard Nixon*, New York, Simon & Schuster, 1978, p. 340.
6. Henry Kissinger, *White House Years*, Boston, Little, Brown and Company, 1979, p. 12.
7. Kalb and Kalb, *Kissinger*, op. cit., p. 26.
8. Nixon, *RN: The Memoirs of Richard Nixon*, op. cit., p. 341.
9. Robert Dallek, *Nixon and Kissinger: Partners in Power*, New York, HarperCollins, 2007, p. 92.
10. Nixon, *RN: The Memoirs of Richard Nixon*, op. cit., p. 478.
11. Scott Shane, 'Robert Dallek on Nixon and Kissinger', *New York Times*, 18 April 2007.

Notes

12 William Morris, *Uncertain Greatness: Henry Kissinger and American Foreign Policy*, New York, Harper & Row, 1977, p. 3.
13 Dallek, *Nixon and Kissinger: Partners in Power*, op. cit., p. 249.
14 Daniel Patrick Moynihan, *A Dangerous Place*, Boston, Little, Brown and Company, 1978, p. 8.
15 Letter from Henry Kissinger to Richard Nixon, 7 April 1971. Personal archives of President Nixon, box 10, Nixon Presidential Library.
16 Isaacson, *Kissinger: A Biography*, op. cit., p. 147.
17 Dallek, *Nixon and Kissinger: Partners in Power*, op. cit., p. 206.
18 Ibid., p. 609.
19 Henry A. Kissinger speaking at Richard Nixon's funeral service, Yorba Linda, California, 27 April 1994.

Paula

1 Walter Isaacson, *Kissinger: A Biography*, New York, Simon & Schuster, 1992, p. 759.
2 Ibid., p. 27
3 Andrew MacKay Scott and Earle Wallace, *Politics, USA: Cases on the American Democratic Process*, New York, Macmillan, 1974, p. 529.
4 Craig R. Whitney, 'Kissinger visits home town, gets big hand', *New York Times*, 16 December 1975.
5 Isaacson, *Kissinger: A Biography*, op. cit., p. 28.
6 Marilyn Berger, 'P. Kissinger, 97, the mother of a statesman', *New York Times*, 16 November 1998.

Realpolitik

1 Stanley Hoffmann, *Primacy or World Order: American Foreign Policy Since the Cold War*, New York, McGraw-Hill, 1978, p. 36.
2 See Robert D. Kaplan, 'Kissinger, Metternich, and Realism', *Atlantic*, June 1999.
3 See John Bew, *Realpolitik: A History*, Oxford, Oxford University Press, 2016.

4 Henry Kissinger, 'The White Revolutionary: reflections on Bismarck', *Daedalus*, summer 1968.
5 Interview with Henry Kissinger, *Der Spiegel*, 6 July 2009.
6 Speech given by Henry Kissinger upon his receipt of the Edmund Burke Award for Service to Culture and Society, 'The limits of universalism', New York, 26 April 2012.
7 John Bew, 'The Kissinger effect on realpolitik', *War on the Rocks*, 29 December 2015.
8 Kissinger, 'The White Revolutionary', op. cit.
9 Henry Kissinger, *A World Restored: Metternich, Castlereagh and the Problems of Peace, 1812–1822*, Boston, Houghton Mifflin, 1957.
10 Lord Byron, *Don Juan* (Dedication), 1819.
11 Kissinger, *A World Restored*, op. cit., p. 326.
12 Henry Kissinger, *World Order*, New York, Penguin Press, 2014, p. 3.
13 Henry Kissinger, *White House Years*, Boston, Little, Brown and Company, 1979, p. 195.
14 Kissinger, *A World Restored*, op. cit., p. 326.
15 Henry Kissinger, *Years of Upheaval*, Boston, Little, Brown and Company, 1982, p. 50.
16 Alexander Hamilton, The Federalist Papers no. 8, 20 November 1787.
17 Stanley Hoffmann, *Dead Ends: American Foreign Policy in the New Cold War*, Cambridge (MA), Ballanger Publishing, 1983, pp. 35–7.

Refugee
1 Walter Isaacson, *Kissinger: A Biography*, New York, Simon & Schuster, 1992, p. 28.
2 Ibid., p. 31.
3 Bernard Gwertzman, 'Now, Kissinger woos his critics', *New York Times*, 19 January 1977.
4 Barnard Law Collier, 'The road to Peking, or, how does this Kissinger do it?', *New York Times*, 14 November 1971.

Notes

5 Ralph Blumenfeld, *Henry Kissinger: The Private and Public Story*, New York, Signet Books, 1974, p. 68–80.
6 Letter written by Henry Kissinger to his parents, 1945 (quoted in Isaacson, *Kissinger: A Biography*, op. cit., p. 51).
7 Isaacson, *Kissinger: A Biography*, op. cit., pp. 56–7.
8 Ibid., p. 29.
9 Ibid., p. 56.

Rockefeller

1 Barnard Law Collier, 'The road to Peking, or, how does this Kissinger do it?', *New York Times*, 14 November 1971.
2 Jeffrey Frank, 'Big spender: Nelson Rockefeller's grand ambitions', *New Yorker*, 6 October 2014.
3 Walter Isaacson, *Kissinger: A Biography*, New York, Simon & Schuster, 1992, p. 91.
4 'Kissinger: the uses and limits of power', *TIME*, 14 February 1969.
5 Jeffrey Goldberg, 'World chaos and world order: conversations with Henry Kissinger', *Atlantic*, 10 November 2016.
6 Isaacson, *Kissinger: A Biography*, op. cit., pp. 137–8.
7 Letter from Richard Nixon to Walter Isaacson, 12 October 1990.
8 Isaacson, *Kissinger: A Biography*, op. cit., p. 501.

Sadat

1 André Fontaine, *Histoire de la détente (1962–1981)*, Paris, Fayard, 1981, p. 436.
2 Anwar el-Sadat, *In Search of Identity: An Autobiography*, New York, HarperCollins, 1978, p. 1.
3 Speech given by Henry Kissinger at the University of Maryland, College Park, 4 May 2000.
4 See Anwar el-Sadat, *In Search of Identity: An Autobiography*, New York, HarperCollins, 1978.
5 Eric Pace, 'Anwar El-Sadat, the daring Arab pioneer of peace with Israel', *New York Times*, 7 October 1981.

Henry Kissinger

6 Edward R. F. Sheehan, 'Why Sadat packed off the Russians', *New York Times*, 6 August 1972.
7 Edward R.F. Sheehan, 'How Kissinger did it: step by step in the Middle East', *Foreign Policy*, 22, spring 1976.
8 Speech given by Anwar Sadat before the People's Assembly, 6 October 1973.
9 Pace, 'Anwar El-Sadat, the daring Arab pioneer of peace with Israel', op. cit.
10 Henry Kissinger, *Years of Upheaval*, Boston, Little, Brown and Company, 1982, p. 646.
11 Ibid., p. 646.
12 el-Sadat, *In Search of Identity*, op. cit., pp. 267–8.
13 Speech given by Henry Kissinger at the University of Maryland, College Park, 4 May 2000.
14 Robert Solé, *Sadate*, Paris, Éditions Perrin, 2013.
15 Interview with Harold H. Saunders by Thomas Stern, *On the Road Again – Kissinger's Shuttle Diplomacy*, Association for Diplomatic Studies and Training, November 1993. Also see Matt Schudel, 'Harold H. Saunders, diplomat in Camp David Accords, Iranian hostage crisis, dies', *Washington Post*, 9 March 2016.
16 Pace, 'Anwar El-Sadat, the daring Arab pioneer of peace with Israel', op. cit.
17 'Mideast Miracle', *TIME*, 10 June 1974.
18 Speech given by Henry Kissinger at the University of Maryland, College Park, 4 May 2000.
19 Interim agreement between Israel and Egypt (Sinai II), 4 September 1975.
20 Kissinger, *Years of Upheaval*, op. cit., p. 650.
21 Speech given by Henry Kissinger at the University of Maryland, College Park, 4 May 2000.

Teacher

1 Raymond Aron, *Memoirs: Fifty Years of Political Reflection* (trans. George Holoch), New York, Holmes & Meier, 1990, p. 386.

Notes

2   Nicolas Baverez, *Raymond Aron: un moraliste au temps des idéologues*, Paris, Flammarion, 2005, p. 224.
3   Henry Kissinger, 'My teacher', *Commentaire*, vol. 8, no. 28–29, February 1985, p. 129.
4   See Raymond Aron, *Memoirs: Fifty Years of Political Reflection* (Foreword by Henry A. Kissinger), New York, Holmes & Meier, 1990.
5   Jean d'Ormesson, *Le vagabond qui passe sous une ombrelle trouée*, Paris, Gallimard, 1978, p. 222.
6   Raymond Aron, *Études politiques*, Paris, Gallimard, 1972, p. 379–80.
7   Raymond Aron, *Penser la guerre, Clausewitz*, vol. I, *L'âge européen*, vol. II, *L'âge planétaire*, Paris, Gallimard, 1976, p. 160 (vol. I).
8   Raymond Aron, 'Les Européens et les deux grands. De quoi avez-vous peur?', *Le Figaro*, 17 August 1973.
9   Raymond Aron, 'Les obscures clartés de Kissinger', *Le Figaro*, 20 December 1972.
10 Raymond Aron, 'La tragédie chilienne', *Le Figaro*, 14 September 1973.
11 NAF 28060, box 207 (Fonds Raymond Aron, BNF). Letter from Raymond Aron to Henry Kissinger of 19 September 1974.

Zhou Enlai

1   See Alistair Horne, *Kissinger: 1973, the Crucial Year*, New York, Simon & Schuster, 2009, p. 70.
2   Henry Kissinger, *White House Years*, Boston, Little, Brown and Company, 1979, pp. 733–44.
3   Memorandum from the President's Assistant for National Security Affairs (Henry Kissinger) to President Nixon, 14 July 1971.
4   Kissinger, *White House Years*, op. cit., pp. 743–9.
5   Henry Kissinger, *On China*, New York, Penguin Press, 2011, p. 241.

6 Richard McGregor, 'Zhou's cryptic caution lost in translation', *Financial Times*, 10 June 2011.
7 On the relationship between Henry Kissinger and Zhou Enlai, see Barbara Keys and Claire Yorke, 'Personal and Political Emotions in the Mind of the Diplomat', *Political Psychology*, 40(6), 2019.
8 Interview with Henry Kissinger by Li Yunfei, *People's Daily*, 18 December 1998.
9 Richard Valeriani, *Travels with Henry*, Boston, Houghton Mifflin, *1979*, p. 89.
10 *TIME*, 26 July 1971.
11 Memorandum from the President's Assistant for National Security Affairs (Henry Kissinger) to President Nixon, 14 July 1971.
12 Kissinger, *On China*, op. cit., pp. 323–4.

Conclusion
1 Fernando Pessoa, *The Book of Disquiet* (trans. Margaret Jull Costa), London, Serpent's Tail, 1991, p. 253.

Epilogue
1 Henry Kissinger, 'How the Ukraine crisis ends', *Washington Post*, 5 March 2014.
2 Ibid.
3 Zbigniew Brzezinski, 'What is to be done? Putin's aggression in Ukraine needs a response', *Washington Post*, 3 March 2014.
4 Georges Pompidou, interview with Richard Nixon, 13 December 1971. Archives of the Secretariat-General of the Presidency of the Republic, technical advisers collection, 5 AG 2 box 1022, France/United States relations, a speech given at the colloquium 'Georges Pompidou et l'Europe' held by the Association Georges Pompidou, 25-26 November 1993, cited in REY Marie-Pierre, *Georges Pompidou, l'Union soviétique et l'Europe* [*Georges Pompidou, the Soviet Union and Europe*], Éditions Complexe 1995, p. 146.

Index

A
Acheson, Dean 118
Adenauer, Konrad 182
Adolphus Busch Hall, Cambridge, Massachusetts 145
AFL-CIO (American Federation of Labor and Congress of Industrial Organizations) 40
Albright, Madeleine ix
Allen, Woody 36
Allende, Salvador 57, 63, 111, 148, 180
Allison, Graham 75
Allon, Yigal 34
Alsop brothers 19
Annie Hall (film) 36
antisemitism ix, 47, 67, 70–71, 122
Arab-Israeli conflict 135–42
Arendt, Hannah 34, 114
Argentina 57
Aron, Raymond 145–9, 170–71
artificial intelligence (AI) 182
al-Assad, Hafez 50, 69, 133, 140
Atherton, Roy 139
Atlantic magazine 130
Austria 92–3
Austro-Hungarian Empire 5
Azcárraga, Emilio 17

B
Bangladesh xi, 55–6, 61–4, 111
baseball 13, 121

Beckenbauer, Franz 16
Beg, M.F.H. 151–2
Begin, Menachem 142
Bergen, Candice 22
Berlin Wall 2, 80
Bew, John 112
Biden, Joe 173
Bilderberg Group 27
Bingham, Jonathan 25
Bismarck, Otto von 5, 9, 36, 89, 112–14, 117
Blatter, Sepp 17
Blood, Archer, 56
Bohemian Club, 27
Bolling, General Alexander R. 84
Book of Disquiet, The (Pessoa) 162
Boston Globe 31
Braden, Tom 19, 21
Brandeis, Louis 70
Brazil football team 14, 18
Brexit referendum 29
Brezhnev, Leonid 14, 40, 44, 133
Brzeziński, Zbigniew ix, 35, 167
Bundy, McGeorge 32, 35–6, 114
Burns, Arthur 70
Burns, Bill 173
Bush, George H.W. 59, 170
Bush, George W. 182
Byron, Lord 115

C
Cairo, Egypt 138, 143

203

Cambodia x, 55, 60–61, 111, 179
Cameron, David 29
Camp Claiborne, Louisiana 83–4, 178
Camp Croft, South Carolina 123, 178
Camp David Accords 142
Carnation Revolution, Portugal (1974) 56
Carter, Jimmy 45, 62, 168, 181
Castlereagh, Viscount *see* Stewart, Robert, Viscount Castlereagh
Castro, Fidel 57, 63
Cayo Alcatraz, Cuba 11
Chamberlain, Neville 76, 116
Chapin, Dwight 97, 99
Chelsea F.C. 14
Chez Tante Louise restaurant, Paris 22
Chile, coup d'état (1973) xi, 57–8, 61, 63, 111, 148, 180
China, People's Republic of 5–6, 20, 61–2, 64–5, 78–9, 114, 151–7, 170, 173, 180
Chomsky, Noam 55
Churchill, Winston 9, 76, 79
City College of New York 123, 177
Clinton, Bill, 27, 130
Clinton, Hillary, 27
Cold War, 35, 45, 59, 116, 156, 160, 179
Colombia 17
Colony Club, New York 25–6
Columbia University, New York 9, 170, 181
Commentaire magazine 146
Concert of Europe 114–15
Conference on Security and Co-operation in Europe, Helsinki 39, 42–3
Confluence journal 34, 114, 145

Congress of Vienna (1814–15) 114, 147
Cosmos soccer team 16
Council on Foreign Relations, New York 35, 179
Critique of Practical Reason (Kant) 32
Critique of Pure Reason (Kant) 32
Cronkite, Walter 25
Crosland, Anthony 14
Cruyff, Johan 13
Cuba 11
    Cuban Missile Crisis (1962) 2, 11
Cushing, Jan 22
Cyprus, coup d'état (1974) 58, 148–9
Czechoslovakia 45

D
Daedalus journal 36
Daily Telegraph 151–2
Dallek, Robert 101
Davidson, Daniel 96
Dayan, Moshe 26, 73
de Gaulle, Charles 1–10, 76, 154, 171, 182
de la Renta, Oscar 27
democracy 54, 78–81
Democratic Party (US) 55
Deng Xiaoping 78, 157
Der Spiegel newspaper 9, 113
Détente, policy of 5–6, 32, 39–40, 42–4, 54, 59, 71–3, 87, 111, 114, 147–8, 156, 170, 180
Diaoyutai State Guesthouse, Beijing 152
Die Zeit 60
DiMaggio, Joe 13
Diplomacy (Kissinger) vii, 58
Disraeli, Benjamin 70
Douglas, Kirk 21, 109
Dulles, John Foster 137, 153

Index

E
Eagleburger, Lawrence 100
East Timor xi, 56–7, 61–2, 65, 111
Eban, Abba 135
Ecevit, Bülent 34
Eggar, Samantha 22
Egypt 51, 104, 133–43, 181
Egypt-Israel Peace Treaty (1979) 142
Ehrlichman, John 102–3
Eisenhower, Dwight D. 4, 7, 129, 179
El Salvador 15
Elliott, William Yandell 31–3, 87, 98, 178
Ertegün, Ahmet 27
Esquire magazine 16
Études politiques (Aron) 147
Europe ix–x, 1–3, 148, 159–63, 171–4
   China and 173
   Concert of Europe 114–15
   European army 1
   European Defence Community 1
   European diplomacy 111–19
   European Economic Community (EEC) 2
   European Union (EU) x, 159–63, 167
   High Representative of the Union for Foreign Affairs and Security Policy 162
   transatlantic relationship 1–6

F
Fahmi, Ismail 51, 136
Faisal, King of Saudi Arabia 69–70
Fallaci, Oriana 23
Farouk I, King of Egypt 133
Ferro, Maurice 8
FIFA 15–17
Figaro, Le 147
Finch, Robert 103
Finland 147, 167
First Indochina War (1946–54) 153
Fleischer, Anneliese (Ann) 36, 178
football 11–18
   United States and 15–18
   World Cup 13, 16–17
Forbidden City, Beijing 155
Ford, Gerald 16, 39–45, 54, 56, 62, 87, 130, 138–9, 181
Foreign Affairs magazine 3
France 1–10, 18, 171
Francis I, Holy Roman Emperor 92–3
Frank, Jean-Michel 127
Frankfurter, Felix 70
Freeman, Chas 154
Fretilin (Revolutionary Front for an Independent East Timor) 56
Friedrich, Carl J. 113
Frost, David 25
Fukuyama, Francis 80, 160
Fürth, Germany 108, 109, 121, 124, 177

G
G.I. Bill (1944), 30
Galbraith, John Kenneth 34
Gallup's most admired men list 25, 181
Gandhi, Indira 64
Garment, Leonard 70
Garrincha 14
Geneva Conference (1954) 152
George Washington High School, New York 121
Georgetown University, Washington 181
Germany 69, 112, 124
   see also Nazi Germany
Gierek, Edward 14
Giscard d'Estaing, Valéry 34
Glenville, Peter 27

205

Henry Kissinger

Gomaa, Sharawi 134
Graham, Katharine 25
Great Britain 115, 119
Greece 58
Gromyko, Andrei, 15
Gulag Archipelago, The (Solzhenitsyn) 39-40

H
Haldeman, H. R, 'Bob' 11, 70, 101, 103
Halperin, Morton 103
Hamilton, Alexander 118
Hanoi, bombing of (1972) 104
Harper's magazine 2
Harvard University 29-37, 86-77, 90-91, 178-9
   Centre for European studies 145
   International Seminar 33-4
   'Kissinger rule' 33
Havel, Václav 45
Havelange, João 17
Hay, John 118
Helms, Jesse 39
Helms, Richard 58
Helsinki Conference (1975) 39-46, 114, 147-8
Herrera, Helenio 12
Hitchens, Christopher 53, 55
Hitler, Adolf 67, 84, 117
Hoffmann, Stanley 35, 36, 111, 118
Honduras 15
Hotel Pierre, New York 97-8
Howar, Barbara 23
Humphrey, Hubert 96
Huntington, Samuel 35
Hussein, King of Jordan 141
Huttenlocher, Daniel 182

I
immigration ix, 122
India-Pakistan conflict 63-5
Indonesia xi, 56-7, 62
Iraq 141
Islamabad, Pakistan 151
Ismail, Hafez 135
Israel 51, 71, 73-4, 91, 104, 135-43

J
Japan 75-6
Jefferson, Thomas 118
Johnson, Lyndon B. 2, 6, 57, 77
Jordan 141

K
Kagame, Paul 80
Kahlo, Frida 95
Kant, Emmanuel 32, 33, 113
Kazakhstan 80
Kennan, George 63, 112
Kennedy, John F. 1, 6, 57, 95, 145
Kent, Connecticut 27, 165, 182
Khan, Yahya 56
Khmer Rouge 55, 60
Kissinger, David (son) 36, 178
Kissinger, Elizabeth (daughter) 36, 178
Kissinger, Henry
   appearance 19
   arrogance and vanity 47-8, 65, 125
   as a refugee 121-5
   birth 177
   business activities 27
   celebrity 19-28
   childhood 11-12, 67-8, 121
   Connecticut estate 165-6
   cunning 91-2
   death 175, 182
   democracy and, 79-81
   education 121-3, 177; *see also* Harvard
   egotism 13, 50, 101, 129
   'ethics of responsibility' 117

Index

fiftieth birthday celebrations, 25, 131–2
German accent, 122
Hollywood and 20–21
intellect/intelligence 47, 85, 103, 137, 146, 161, 178
Jewishness 51–2, 67–74, 122
Machiavellianism 29–30, 112, 117
marriage to Ann 36
marriage to Nancy 25–7
mentors 31–3, 83–8, 98, 127–32
military power and 116
military service 69, 83–5, 123–4, 178
national security advisor 1, 98–9, 130, 179–80
personality, 48–9, 51, 65–6, 99–102
realism and 46, 114–19
secretary of state 28–9, 70, 74, 180
secretary of state 29
sense of humour 47–52
vilification of, 53–66
Washington apartment 24
womanising and playboy reputation 21–4, 49–50
see also Harvard University; *Realpolitik*
Kissinger, Louis (father)12, 67–8, 86, 107–10, 122, 174, 177
Kissinger, Nancy 25–7, 69, 87, 165–7, 169, 181
Kissinger, Paula (mother) 12, 107–10, 128, 174, 177
Kissinger, Walter (brother) 107, 177
Kissinger Associates 27, 181–2
Klein, Herb 103
Korean Peninsula 153
Kraemer, Fritz 32, 83–8, 98–9, 113, 125, 178
Kristallnacht 121, 124
Kwa Geok Choo 172

L

La Casa Pacifica, San Clemente, California 20, 23
Lafayette College, Pennsylvania, 69, 178
Laos, bombing campaign x, 60, 179
Lê Đức Thọ 180
Leadership: Six Studies in World Strategy (Kissinger) 182
Lee Kuan Yew 75–82, 172, 182
Leutershausen, Germany 12
Lion, Menahem 121, 124
Lodge Jr, Henry Cabot 59
Los Angeles, 20
Los Angeles Times 12
Luce, Clare Boothe 95
Luce, Henry 95

M

Maginnes, Nancy *see* Kissinger, Nancy
Makarios III, Archbishop and president of Cyprus 58, 149
Mao Zedong 5, 152–4, 155, 157
Marsh, Jack 39
Marshall, George 118
'Meaning of history: reflections on Spengler, Toynbee and Kant, The' (dissertation), 33, 50, 89, 92, 113, 178
Meir, Golda 73, 74, 100, 133, 136, 139
Memoirs (Aron) 145
Memoirs (Nixon) 6
Metternich, Klemens von x, 34, 50, 89–93, 114, 117, 160
Mexico 17
Middle East 7, 51, 133–43, 181
Miller, Ann 23
Mitterrand, François 159
'Moral foundations of foreign policy, The' (speech), 43

Henry Kissinger

Morgenthau, Hans J. 34, 112–14
Moynihan, Daniel Patrick 72–3, 102
Murdoch, Rupert 27
Mussolini, Benito 84

N
Nakasone, Yasuhiro 34
Napoleon Bonaparte 91
Nasser, Gamal Abdel 133, 138
Nathia Gali, Pakistan 152
National Commission on Terrorist Attacks Upon the United States (9-11 Commission) 182
National Security Council 97–8
NATO (North Atlantic Treaty Organisation) 1–2, 167–8
Nazarbayev, Nursultan 80
Nazi Germany 12, 67, 86, 92
  denazification viii, 13, 30, 124
Necessity for Choice: Prospects of American Foreign Policy (Kissinger) 179
Nessen, Ron 41
Netherlands football team 13
New York, 26–7
New York Times 18, 31, 48, 151
Newsweek 20
Niebuhr, Reinhold 112–13
Night (Wiesel) 68–9
Nitze, Paul 114
Nixon, Pat 100
Nixon, Richard 11, 14, 19–20, 23–4, 48, 92–3, 95–105, 109, 138–9, 154, 182
  antisemitism 70–71, 102–3
  China and 62, 79, 153–6, 180
  de Gaulle and 1, 4–8
  ideology and 116
  India and 64
  Kissinger and 95–105, 130–31, 169–70, 179

Kissinger's playboy reputation and 24–5
  Pompidou and 171
  Vietnam War and 55, 60
  Watergate scandal, 103, 136, 181
Nobel Peace Prize viii, 45, 142, 180
Nol, Lon 60
nuclear weapons 36, 48, 117, 179
Nuclear Weapons and Foreign Policy (Kissinger) 36, 96, 179
Nuremberg Laws 177

O
Obama, Barack 79
On China (Kissinger) 182
One Day in the Life of Ivan Denisovich (Solzhenitsyn), 41
Opium of the Intellectuals, The (Aron) 146
d'Ormesson, Jean 146, 159

P
Pakistan x, 55–6, 63–5, 151–2
Palestine 141
Palmerston, Lord *see* Temple, Henry John, 3rd Viscount Palmerston
Panama Canal 118
Paris, France 1–2, 22
Paris Peace Accords 111, 180
Partial Test Ban Treaty (1963) 1
Peace of Westphalia (1648) 115
Pelé 15–16, 41
Peres, Shimon 51, 73, 91
Persico, Joseph 129
Pessoa, Fernando 162
Peterson, Peter G. 102
Phnom Penh, Vietnam 2
Pinochet, Augusto xi, 57–8, 63, 180
Pisar, Samuel 40
Playboy Clubs 21
Pol Pot 55, 61

Index

Poland 14, 45
Pompidou, Georges 171–2
Portugal, 56
Putin, Vladimir 166–8, 173

Q
Quinn, Sally 21

R
Rabin, Yitzhak 51, 73, 91, 142
RAND Corporation, 20
Reagan, Ronald 28, 43–5, 54, 59, 130, 143
Realpolitik x, 35, 43, 54, 61, 100, 111–19, 156–7, 159–60
Reinsurance Treaty (1887–90) 5
Republican Party (US) 45, 54
Richelieu, Cardinal de 58
Rive Gauche bistro, Washington 21
Rochau, August Ludwig von 112, 119
Rockefeller, John D. 131
Rockefeller, Nelson 25–6, 32, 35–6, 87, 96–9, 101, 109, 127–32, 179, 181
Rogers, William 48, 101, 103, 135, 137
Roosevelt, Theodore 118
Rose al-Youssef magazine 138
Ross, Steven 16
Rusk, Dean 128, 137
Russia 2–3, 5–6, 11, 14, 165–9
  Moscow–Beijing axis 173
  see also Soviet Union
Russo-Japanese War (1904–5) 118
Russo-Ukrainian War 165–9
Rwanda 80

S
Sabri, Ali 134
Sadat, Anwar 51, 73, 133–43, 154, 172–3, 181–2
Safire, William 49, 70

SALT I (Strategic Arms Limitations Talks) agreement)1972) 180
Saunders, Harold H. 139
Schlesinger, Arthur 121
Schlesinger, James 87
Schmidt, Eric 182
Scowcroft, Brent 181
Shklar, Judith N. 35
'shuttle diplomacy' 139–41
Sinai Interim Agreement (1975) 141
Singapore, 75–7, 79–82, 172
Sino–American Rapprochement 111
Six-Day War (1967) 135
soccer *see* football
social media 161
Solidarność movement 45
Solzhenitsyn, Aleksandr 39–42
Sook Ching (Singapore massacre and purge) 76
Soviet Union 14–15, 39–41, 44, 59–60, 71–2, 87, 147, 156
  China and 153, 156
  Cold War 35, 45, 59, 116, 156, 160, 179
  Egypt and 133–4
  Soviet Jews 71–3
  see also Détente; Russia; Solzhenitsyn
Special Studies Project 129
Spengler, Oswald 33, 113
Sports Illustrated 18
SpVgg Fürth football team 12–13, 17
St John, Jill 22
Standard Oil 127
Stern, Falk 108
Stewart, Robert, Viscount Castlereagh, 34, 89, 114–15, 117, 119, 160
Stimson, Henry 118

209

'Strains on the Alliance' (Kissinger) 3
Suharto 56–7, 62, 65
Syria 104, 135, 140, 181

T
Taiwan 154
Talleyrand (Charles-Maurice de Talleyrand-Périgord), vii, 160
Teller, Edward 128
Temple, Henry John, 3rd Viscount Palmerston, 119
Thatcher, Margaret 182
Thiệu, Nguyễn Văn 91
Thirty Years' War (1618–48) 115
Thurmond, Strom 39
TIME magazine 140, 155
Tindemans, Leo 34
Toynbee, Arnold J. 33, 113
Trade Act (US, 1974) 72
Trader Vic's, Los Angeles 22–3
Trudeau, Pierre 32
Truman, Harry 97

U
Ukraine 165–9, 175
Ullmann, Liv 22
University of Maryland 134
Urban VIII, Pope 58
USSR *see* Soviet Union

V
Vagabond qui passe sous une ombrelle trouée, Le (d'Ormesson) 146
Videla, Jorge Rafael 57
Vietnam
　North Vietnam 20, 22, 55, 61, 156, 180
　Paris Peace Accords 111, 180
　South Vietnam 55, 60, 62, 148, 180
　US withdrawal 59–62
Vietnam War (1955–75) 7, 23, 45, 54–5, 77, 91, 93, 179–80

W
Wałęsa, Lech 45
Wallace, Mike 25
Walters, Barbara 22
Walters, Vernon 4
Washington Heights, New York 12, 27, 68, 177
Washington, DC 19–20
Washington Post 21, 25, 167–8
Watergate scandal, 103
White House Years (Kissinger) 181
Wiesel, Elie 68
Wilson, Woodrow 112, 118
Winchester, Lucy 24–5
Winter Olympics (Beijing, 2022) 173
Women's Wear Daily journal 22
World Order (Kissinger) 182
World Restored: Metternich, Castlereagh and the Problems of Peace, A (thesis) 34–5, 114, 178
World War II (1939–45) 3, 30, 69, 85–6
Wouk, Herman 70

X
Xi Jinping 78, 173

Y
Yom Kippur War (1973) 73, 91, 104, 111, 135–8, 141, 181
Yugoslavia 160

Z
Zavidovo, Russia 14
Zhou Enlai 137, 151–7, 172, 180
Zionism 72–3